For Grandma—I miss you.

THINK OUTSIDE

THE CELL

An Entrepreneur's Guide for the Incarcerated and Formerly Incarcerated

JOSEPH ROBINSON

RESILIENCE
MULTIMEDIA

CONTENTS

Foreword by Steve Mariotti 7

Acknowledgements 11

Introduction 13

Part I: On the Come-Up 19
chapter 1 CHANGE YOUR MIND CHANGE YOUR LIFE 21

chapter 2 THINK BIG...START SMALL 33

chapter 3 ABOUT THEM BENJAMINS 49

chapter 4 LEVERAGE YOUR VISION 75

Part 2: Getting Down to Business 87
chapter 5 LAWS OF THE LAND 89

chapter 6 WHY BUSINESSES FAIL 99

chapter 7 YOUR GAME PLAN 103

chapter 8 CHOOSING THE RIGHT BUSINESS STRUCTURE . 107

chapter 9 SOCIAL ENTREPRENEURSHIP 119

chapter 10 BEING YOUR OWN BOSS 125

chapter 11 FLOODING THE MARKET 127

Part 3: Money Matters 135
chapter 12 CASH RULES 137

chapter 13 BANK ON IT 145

chapter 14 CREDIT MATTERS 147

chapter 15 KEEPING TRACK OF YOUR MONEY 159

chapter 16 TAXES GALORE 167

chapter 17 MANAGING RISK 175

chapter 18 GIVE AND TAKE 179

chapter 19 DOTTING "I's" AND CROSSING "T's" 181

chapter 20 INTELLECTUAL PROPERTY 189

chapter 21 MAKE IT HAPPEN 195

Appendix A: Business Resources 201

Appendix B: Recommended Reading 207

Appendix C: Legislative Committees on Small Business 213

Appendix D: NY State Occupational Licensing Survey 230

Appendix E: IRS Publications and Forms 253

Appendix F: Business Tax Deductions 255

Index 267

About the Author 271

FOREWORD

I KNOW FIRSTHAND THAT ENTREPRENEURSHIP has the potential to redirect—and even save —lives. Teaching entrepreneurship has certainly changed my life, and reading and applying the information contained in this book is sure to change yours.

My journey to teaching entrepreneurship started indirectly. One day in 1981, while jogging in a park near the East River, three young men approached me and asked for ten dollars. When I answered that I didn't have any money, they pushed me to the ground and kicked me. It was a traumatic experience, and I went into therapy. I couldn't understand why these kids would risk going to prison for a few bucks. They must have had other means of making a living. After all, we lived in the wealthiest country in history.

My therapist convinced me to confront my fears head-on. To this end, I decided to become a teacher in the kind of neighborhoods that those young men had come from. I needed to know what motivated these kids to waste their youthful potential in committing crimes. I gave up my import-export business and went to work for the Board of Education, assigned (at my request) to teach in the toughest high schools in New York City.

Within hours of my first assignment, teaching math at Boys and Girls High School in Bedford-Stuyvesant, in Brooklyn, I discovered that many of my 10th- and 11th-grade students hadn't even mastered what they should have learned in junior high school. I noticed, too, that many of them were extremely materialistic, sporting all manner of designer sneakers, high-fashion clothing, and jewelry. So I decided to bring inexpensive watches and other trinkets to class as props for math lessons. This reality-based approach got their attention, and my students began to grasp concepts that up until then they had struggled with.

School administrators complained that I was putting too much emphasis on money and material things. But I knew better; the changed attitudes and improved grades of my students convinced me that I was onto something. I came to understand that the boys who robbed me, and countless others like them, felt trapped in a no-way-out economic trap that made them desperate.

In 1986, I left the public school system to establish a nonprofit organization based on my perceptions. The National Foundation for Teaching Entrepreneurship (NFTE) was established in the following year. Over time, I developed unique methodologies and curricula to inspire low-income young people to start their own businesses.

Two decades later, NFTE's programs are thriving in 22 states, and 14 countries in Europe, Asia and Africa. We have had over 200,000 graduates. NFTE is at the forefront of an international movement to introduce economically at-risk youth to the power of ownership.

Joe Robinson—both a friend and an inspiration—understands the potential of entrepreneurship. A visionary with uncommon tenacity, he has turned the circumstances of his life around and made them work to his advantage. He refused to be held back by his criminal past or prison experiences. I admire his unwavering focus and determination, not to mention his first-rate leadership ability.

With *Think Outside the Cell*, Joe has tapped into the hopes, aspirations, and fears of incarcerated and formerly incarcerated individuals everywhere. It hasn't been lost on him that they, too, want to take part in the American Dream. They, too, want to be productive, law-abiding and whole members of society. This book will show them how, in a direct yet highly readable step-by-step manner.

Think Outside the Cell is more than a business book. It is an empowerment guide for everyone who has been, at one time or another, enmeshed in the criminal justice system—locked out of mainstream society. Joe pulls no punches; he makes no excuses for the self-destructive attitudes and behaviors that drive people to commit crimes. Instead, he holds his readers accountable, convincingly urging them to take responsibility for their actions and lives.

With over two million men and women held in state and federal prisons (and millions more under some form of control or monitoring) this book could not have come at a better time.

I firmly believe that entrepreneurship is the best-kept secret to addressing many of the social maladies we currently face as a nation. This book will play an important role in sharing that secret for generations to come. I urge you to read it.

Steve Mariotti,
Founder and President, NFTE

ACKNOWLEDGEMENTS

WHILE I DON'T PROFESS to be religious, I do believe in a higher power. God, if you will. And without God's presence in my life, there's no way this book could have been possible.

I thank my mother, Mary Louise Robinson, for instilling in me an unshakable belief in myself. You were so right: I can do anything that I put my mind to. Thank you, Ma. For everything.

This book also would not have been possible without my loving and supportive wife, Sheila Rosita Rule. Thanks so much for editing the various drafts of my book, and for encouraging me to walk my prayer. To do the damn thing. You are an amazing woman, a gift of a wife. As my literary mentor, you inspire me to express my higher self so that I touch people through the written word.

Mark and Jan Folsom, thank you for never giving up on me! I put you through hell, as I tried to find my way in life. You were by my side all along, never losing hope in the goodness that resides in me. You've taught me the meaning of genuine friendship.

Marsha Roschelle Rule, my sister-in-law, your meticulous editing and helpful content suggestions helped make this book a coherent and engaging read. Thanks so much.

My dear friend and mentor, Steve Mariotti, thanks for believing in me and agreeing to write the foreword to this book. It means the world to me.

Dr. Garry A. Mendez, thank you for providing an exemplary model of African manhood, and for demonstrating what selfless leadership is all about.

Thanks also goes to Derrick "Ras Sunda" Hamilton for capturing my vision for this book, and drawing such a powerful front cover.

Thanks, bro.

Stanley "Jamel" Bellamy, thanks for deciphering my sometimes cryptic handwriting and typing the first three chapters of my manuscript. You've been more helpful to me than you realize.

INTRODUCTION

IN A NATION OBSESSED with money and materialism, it should not surprise you that most crimes (white-collar or otherwise) are committed out of a real or imagined need for money, or the things money can buy. Robbery, burglary, drug selling and, in many cases, even murder and manslaughter all point to a reckless pursuit of the almighty dollar.

Point blank, you were not born to commit crimes; you were not predisposed to commit vicious and antisocial acts. And a life in and out of jail and prison is certainly not what your parents had in mind for your future. Granted, the hardscrabble environments you grew up in may have lacked positive role models to show you a better way to realize your dreams of success. Without consistent exposure to positive mentors, it might have been easy for you to fall victim to the alluring traps of get-rich-quick schemes. Without mentors to help broaden your scope to the countless options available to you in life, it became almost second nature to think (and believe) that you had no choice but to rob people, that you had no choice but to sell drugs, no choice but to do whatever it was that led you to prison.

The truth is, even when your options seem minimal or nonexistent, you always have choices. No one made you sell drugs. No one made you burglarize people's homes or businesses. For whatever reason, you made a choice to commit crimes. Misguided, flawed, perhaps conditioned, but a choice nonetheless.

The ability to make choices is both a gift from God and a responsibility to yourself and others. Making wise and well-thought-out choices is the single most important ability that you and I have. I say this because whether we weigh our options or not, we have to live with the consequences of the choices we make every day. Our thoughts, and the actions that derive from them, do not exist in a vacuum. There is a domino effect, a chain reaction: thought, action, consequence; thought, action, consequence; you get the idea.

Why am I talking about choices when this book is supposed to be about business, you might be asking yourself. Make no mistake about it, this book *is* about business. Specifically, it's about how you can help your loved ones start a successful small business — while you are *still* in prison. And it's about investing in your business knowledge so that you can create your own job when you are paroled, instead of hoping that someone is compassionate and open-minded enough to give you a job.

At the same time, this book *is* about the choices we make throughout life. It's about choosing a different value system, one that aims to help others instead of hurting them, a value system that honors human dignity and worth. This book is about choosing a better life for yourself and your loved ones. It's about being the best **you** that you can be. Remember, no one is going to make you do anything. The choice of living a rewarding life is yours to make. Yours and yours alone.

* * *

From the outset of my incarceration in 1992, I made a conscious choice to make the most out of my time in prison. Determined to return home to my fiancée and my then two-year-old son, I spent several hours every day researching procedural, substantive and case law in an effort to have my murder conviction overturned or modified. It was during this early stage in my 25-to-life sentence that I began reflecting on how much money I'd made selling drugs — and how much I'd wasted.

The reality was that when I was arrested I had little to show for risking my life day in and day out. I had little to show for all the days and weeks I had spent out of town — away from my family. Not only did I *not* own a home, and *not* have enough money for good legal representation, I essentially left my fiancée to fend for herself.

The weight of this realization kept me up many a night. I knew there had to be a better way.

In 1994, while in Elmira Correctional Facility (in Elmira, New York), I began reading every book I could get my hands on that had anything to do with personal finance and business. One after another, I devoured these books, magazines and newsletters. I reread some, took notes from others, and purchased still others to add to my personal library. In these books, I saw a way out of a life of crime, and a way out of the projects. I envisioned a life without having to look over my shoulders for police, a life filled with dream homes, dream cars and dream vacations with my family.

Indeed, the countless business and personal finance books that I've read throughout the course of my incarceration have greatly expanded the range of business and life options I imagine for myself upon release from prison. I've learned how to turn my passions into businesses, how to write a winning business plan, how to legally maximize business tax deductions, how to hire the right employees and managers, and how to invest in stocks, bonds, real estate and mutual funds. I've also learned about the spiritual and social rewards of giving back to my community — and causes that I am passionate about. Trust me, if you apply yourself, you can accomplish so much.

I still have vivid dreams of living the good life. A good and, hopefully, long life. The difference now is that I no longer focus on money and material things alone. I now understand that money is a means to an end, not the end itself. Money is a tool to be used for your own good and for the good of others. It's a tool that provides options, choices. For instance, having a sufficient amount of money gives you the options of good health insurance, a good education for your children, and time to spend with loved ones.

Yet, as beneficial and enlightening as the books on entrepreneurship have been, none of them addressed the wealth of possibilities available to incarcerated and formerly incarcerated persons who want to start their own business when they are released. There were also no books to guide those who wanted to start a business while their loved ones were still in prison. None of the books talked about the regulatory and/or parole restrictions that might hinder this population from

either starting a business or securing a particular license because of
their felony convictions. Finally, none of the books I read addressed
the often negative and counterproductive value systems that many
incarcerated persons hold. Nor did they address the sense of
hopelessness, victimhood and disconnect from mainstream America
that too many people in jails and prisons embrace.

* * *

I began teaching incarcerated men (as well as my loved ones
via letters and visits) about entrepreneurship and investing in 1995.
Now, seldom does a day go by without someone asking me a question
about business or investing. I've witnessed an undeniable hunger in
incarcerated people to learn about legitimate ways to make money. It
is, after all, a reason why you are reading this book. Let's face it: one
way or another, you will have to make a living when you get out. You'll
either: 1) own your own business; 2) work for someone else; 3) collect
Social Security checks or welfare; or 4) commit crimes to feed, clothe
and house yourself.

Recently, while facilitating a class on entrepreneurship, I had an
epiphany. If I wanted to read a book on entrepreneurship written
specifically for incarcerated persons, I would have to write it myself.
I became enthused because the idea of writing a book spoke to my
belief that business is not only about money; it's about people. That is,
if you put people's wants and needs first, you are almost guaranteed to
be successful in business. I also thoroughly enjoy helping others.

I earnestly hope that you will be inspired — and moved to action
— by the wealth of information contained within these pages, that
you'll begin thinking *outside* the cell.

ORGANIZATION OF THIS BOOK

Think Outside the Cell is divided into three parts. Part I — "On the Come-Up" — consists of the first four chapters and deals primarily with making real but incremental changes in one's thinking and lifestyle. Included is a chapter on saving and investing (chapter 3: About Them Benjamins); one on how to get others to embrace your dreams (chapter 4: Leverage Your Vision).

Chapters five through eleven form the basis of Part II: "Getting Down to Business." This part encompasses the fundamental aspects of actually starting and operating a business.

Part III consists of chapters twelve through twenty-one: "Money Matters."

PART I
ON THE COME-UP

chapter 1

CHANGE YOUR MIND
CHANGE YOUR LIFE

LET'S FACE IT, CHANGE is daunting. Going from the familiar to the unfamiliar takes a lot of courage. Even when things don't work out the way we want, many of us would rather stay put than try something new or do something differently. We'll complain about not being happy in a relationship, complain about not being treated fairly or with respect, complain about how much time the judge sentenced us to, etc., etc. Other than complain — and walk around like you've got rocks in your jaw — what else do you do? If you're like most people, you don't do anything. Except complain.

You keep complaining about how bad you've got it and how rough your upbringing was, as if complaining will make things better. As if it will make your problems go away. It won't. Trust me when I tell you. Without the courage to act, to do something about your situation, nothing will change.

You've heard the saying about insanity. It goes: Insanity is doing the same thing over and over while expecting a different result. If this sounds like how you've been behaving, it's time you take a hard look at how you think and operate.

The judge who sentenced you may not be the only one who's keeping you in prison. *You* may be keeping yourself in prison. Negative attitudes about life will hold you back — and keep you locked up in a mental prison. A prison filled with hatred, despair, anger, jealousy, pessimism and a sense of victimhood. A prison that, if you allow it, will follow you home when you are eventually paroled from the physical prison that now houses you.

For all intents and purposes, you are being held against your will while confined to a prison cell or dormitory. Others dictate when you eat, sleep, shower, exercise, etc. You have very little choice in the matter. You either play by the rules or deal with the consequences.

Control over your thoughts is quite another thing. Unless you allow others to do so, no one can control your mind. No one can dictate what you think or how you think. You have complete authority over your mind — and its immense power. It is a proven fact: if you want to change your life, you must first change your mind!

CHANGE REQUIRES COURAGE

Courage is not the absence of fear. It's the exact opposite. Courage is being afraid to change, but making the necessary changes anyway. Or at least being able to admit that you need to change. It's breaking away from so-called friends and homeys (and sometimes even loved ones) because you realize that they are holding you back from accomplishing your goals. This takes heart, which, by the way, is the meaning of courage.

Courage also means standing up to peer pressure. Young adults and teenagers are not the only ones confronted by this. Prisons and jails are rampant with peer pressure, a follow-the-crowd mentality. Nowadays everyone seems to be a thug, a gangster. Racial and ethnic divisions and strife persist because people lack the courage to be their own person. Afraid of being perceived as soft, they project false images of being tough and insensitive. You know, like I do, that when you're alone in the cell at night you feel pain, sadness, remorse. But so much time and energy is invested in projecting a thug, tough-guy image that it's often difficult establishing meaningful relationships in prison. Getting to the core of an individual becomes work-intensive.

Change will not become a reality until you exercise courage. Until you decide to keep it real with yourself.

CHANGE REQUIRES DETERMINATION

Because humans are creatures of habit, it will not be easy to simply change how you think. It will not be at all easy to change what you do with your time, what you do with your life. Exercising the courage to change is the first step, but without determination it is quite possible that your change will be short lived. Just think about how hard it is for people to quit smoking cigarettes. Even when smokers are aware that throat or lung cancer runs in their families, many of them will continue smoking. They'll make New Year's resolution after New Year's resolution to quit smoking once and for all, only to kick themselves in the butt a few months (or days) later for picking the nasty habit back up. While they had the courage or desire to change, they did not have the determination, the willpower and the inner strength to stick to their goal. Change cannot be just some nice-sounding cliché. In order for change to be real, in order for it to take root, you must be determined to make change a part of your life.

CHANGE REQUIRES VISION

By vision I mean seeing yourself in a better station in life. If you don't envision change you will not likely experience it.

I read somewhere that everything happens twice: first in your mind, then in the physical realm. Make a habit of seeing yourself as a business person, seeing yourself as successful in all aspects of life and, finally, seeing yourself as a changed person. You are what you think.

CHANGE REQUIRES HOPE

Why hope? Because it is hope, the feeling that what you desire will be realized, that acts as a motivation for you to do what's necessary to make change a reality. Hope fuels your desire for real change, be it internal or external. It makes your efforts seem worthwhile.

When I talk about change requiring hope, I'm not talking about wishful thinking. Hope without action doesn't amount to much. If all you do is hope that your circumstances will change, if all you do is hope that you'll eliminate bad habits, then nothing will come of it. You must take action. You must do something — or stop doing something — in order for change to manifest.

CHANGE REQUIRES FAITH

There are no guarantees that a change in your thinking or behavior will bring about a desired result. Often it will. But sometimes it won't. This is where faith comes in. Not necessarily a religious faith, but a faith that's based simply on a belief that your act of courage, your determination, vision and hope, will reap dividends. That it will pay off.

Faith, like hope, is an incredible motivator. It puts the wind at your back, propelling you forward. Faith allows you to step out of your old, unproductive — even self-destructive — thinking patterns and behaviors, knowing in your gut that you are going to be just fine. That what you're doing, or have stopped doing, is the right thing. Genuine change demands nothing less than an abiding faith that you can become the person you want to be, that you can have what you want in life, that you can do whatever you put your mind to.

Believe that change is possible.

Earlier I talked about being locked up in a mental prison. The self-imposed kind that holds you back from moving ahead in life. The only way to free yourself from this prison of the mind is to reinvent yourself. No, I'm not talking about cloning yourself. And I'm certainly not talking about getting a surgical operation like John

Travolta did to himself and Nicholas Cage in the movie "Face Off." Not that kind of reinventing.

The kind of reinventing I'm talking about is going from a personal, familial and social liability to an asset. From a so-called thug to an agent for positive change.

Prior to my incarceration, my time and energy were split (not evenly, I might add) between being a family man and college student on the one hand, and a drug dealer on the other. I straddled the fence in a way that I've come to realize was schizophrenic. While out on the streets running my drug operation, I wore my game face. I took no crap. But even while in the drug game I had a certain compassion for people. I hurt people, yet there was a soft, humane side of me that was undeniable. The fact that I had uncles — and a few peers — that had succumbed to the scourge of the crack epidemic meant that I always saw people, even if they smoked crack, as people. I didn't see customers as less than human beings. And I didn't treat them as less than human beings.

At the same time, whenever I was home with my son and his mother, I brought with me a certain toughness. I didn't realize it then, but the callousness of the streets had changed the way I treated my son's mother. I became distant, hardened, demanding. More than a few arguments, and fights, were started because of my emotional changes, and because of the amount of time I was spending away from home.

It wasn't until I got arrested in March 1992 and struggled through long, lonely hours of reflection that I was able to see — and appreciate — how conflicted and confused I was about my role in life. How unfocused I was in terms of my goals in life. I was a mess. But I was able to acknowledge that I needed to get my act together.

Like 50 Cent said toward the end of his "In Tha Club" track, *I'm focused, man!*

From then on, I vowed to myself and my then fiancée that I would no longer try to live a double life, that of a family man and college student, and that of a drug dealer. I vowed to reinvent myself. To make time serve me, as Don King said about his 3 ½ - year stint in the 60's for manslaughter.

I knew this would mean that some people would consider me soft, lame. But it was the price I'd have to pay in order to truly reinvent myself. I could not worry about how others would perceive me. I would live my life for me.

There's no way I could serve anyone else's time but my own (not that I'd want to!), so how I thought and how I lived my life was my decision alone.

Diligently working on my case was a given. I was granted permission for special access to the law library. Five days out of the week (sometimes seven) I was there, researching the law as it applied to my case.

But I wanted to do more than just get out of prison. I wanted to stay out of prison. Since I'd already decided that I would reinvent myself, I knew I had to read books that would facilitate my conversion. To start with, I had to learn who I was as a black man, so I read books like Dr. Na'im Akbar's "Vision for Blackmen," Malcolm X's autobiography, George G. M. James's "Stolen Legacy" and Chancellor Williams' "Destruction of Black Civilization." Once I had fed my hunger to learn what black people have endured over the past five-hundred-plus years, how much we have achieved and how much we have yet to accomplish, I began reading books on personal finance and entrepreneurship. Books like "Money In Your Mailbox" and "Multiple Streams of Income," both by Robert G. Allen; "Think and Grow Rich: A Black Choice" by Dennis Kimbro; "The Millionaire Mind" by Thomas Stanley and, later, "Rich Dad, Poor Dad" (and other books in the "Rich Dad" series) by Robert Kiyosaki. The countless business biographies I've read have spared me a bunch of avoidable mistakes and further helped me to see myself as a successful business man.

FEAR

The reason most people don't even make an effort to change (either the way they think, how they behave or the quality of their lives) is because of a four-letter word: Fear.

Point blank, if you do not overcome your fear of rejection, fear of failure, or even fear of success, you will not get ahead in life. You will remain in prison. A mental prison, that is.

No one likes to be rejected. It's simply not a good feeling. But guess what; when you excitedly tell others about your million-dollar business idea and they reject it, it's not the end of the world. Their rejection won't kill you. And it's important to understand that they're rejecting the idea — not you. They may reject your idea for a number of reasons. Perhaps you didn't explain the business idea, product or service well enough. You may have to do your homework so you can better convey the idea. Maybe you lacked passion and enthusiasm when trying to sell them on the idea. Or maybe they're plain jealous that you're taking charge of your life. Whatever, there is no reason to fear rejection. Instead, use it as a learning opportunity. Rejection and failure are part of the journey to success. They come with the territory.

If possible, ask people why they don't believe in your business idea, product or service. Ask how you can improve on it, even how you can improve your presentation. No matter what, do not become discouraged simply because someone is unable to envision your dream. It is, after all, your dream, your million-dollar idea.

The same goes for fear of failure (or success). Failure won't kill you. In fact, failure is part of the process of becoming successful. You will not succeed in life without failing, not once but on numerous occasions. And while it may seem odd that some people actually fear success, it's true. For some people, success means added responsibilities, responsibilities they'd rather do without. Others believe that they'll lose themselves, their personalities, if they become successful. Some people fear how they will be perceived by others, and still others believe they are not worthy of success.

We learn by doing — by making mistakes and learning from them. Unfortunately, "failure" has been given a bum rap. When people hear the word failure, they often think of someone who's down on their luck, someone who's washed up, out of the game of life. The truth is that any successful person you can think of (or know) has failed again and again. The difference between them and those who are washed up and out of the game of life is that successful people get back up when they're knocked down. They dust themselves off, learn from their mistakes (failure) and use what they learn to get ahead.

Your being in prison does not make you a failure. The only thing that can make you a failure is if you give in to fear of rejection, failure or success, if you don't learn from your mistakes, your bad choices, or if you quit the game of life. You can succeed in life — no matter the circumstances you find yourself in.

INCREASE YOUR CONTENT, EXPAND YOUR CONTEXT

Changing your mind in order to change your life can be summed up in a two-step process. I'd love to be able to say that I originated this brilliantly simplified process, but it belongs to none other than Robert T. Kiyosaki, the author of "Rich Dad, Poor Dad" and other books in the "Rich Dad" series (and "Rich Dad's Advisors" series), and a man I consider a mentor, although we've never met.

I read about this concept in his book "Retire Young, Retire Rich." And it has stuck with me ever since. In short, this concept is about not only acquiring the knowledge and skills necessary to take you to the next level. It's about changing your mindset, expanding your context, from a poverty and scarcity mentality to a wealth and abundance mentality. Here's how I interpreted and personalized this simple yet profound concept.

Step One: Increase Your Content

Essentially, step one requires you to read, listen to audiotapes, attend classes, etc. It boils down to getting educated by formal and informal means. For many incarcerated people this is the easy part. With nothing but time on your hands, you probably read at least a book a week, or at least a book a month. That's more than most people on the outside can say, with their busy and hectic lives.

Learn all you can now because when you're paroled, you won't have the same amount of "free" time to read as you do now. The key, though, is to read nonfiction books (and magazines and newspapers) that will add to your knowledge. Increasing your content is like filling up the proverbial glass that's half full.

Step Two: Expand Your Context

Expanding your context means adopting a new set of values. It means changing your perspective, your outlook on things. Unlike step one, this crucial step is not so easy to accomplish. But it is possible.

Why do I say this step isn't easy to carry out? All you have to do is look around (or even at yourself) to see people resisting change — genuine, internal change. By this I mean people clinging to behaviors and attitudes from their youth. These are people with arrested development. You know the type: they're in their late 30s, early 40s with their pants hanging off their behinds; they lack self-control and wind up in heated, one-upmanship arguments and fights, or they go around calling themselves Gangsta, Murder or Trouble.

If content is what goes into or fills your half-full glass, then context is the funnel that directs the flow of the content. It's the lens through which you see yourself and experience people and life.

I don't care how many books you've read, how many degrees you've earned or correspondence courses you've taken, if your context — your reality — has not changed, then you will be confined to the limits of your frame of reference.

Here's an example of what I'm talking about. Do you know of people who can accurately quote — word for word — from the Bible or Quran, who can elaborate on a particular historical event with such passion and vividness as to make you feel that you are reliving it, but whose behavior and attitudes do not reflect or correspond with their seeming intellectual abilities? Of course you do. We all know people like that. They try to impress others by wearing their knowledge on their sleeves. And yet, on a deeper level, they haven't changed. They haven't grown up. Their book smarts make them appear intelligent on the surface. But on the inside, where it really counts, they continue to embrace a criminal and thug mentality. Until they expand their context and begin to see themselves as more than criminals, more than inmates, prisoners or convicts, they will remain liabilities — to themselves, their loved ones and society.

The Cultural Equation

Just how does one change his thinking and, by extension, his behavior? In a word, values. At the root of all behavior are one's values. When you change your mind you in effect change your values. By values I mean your established ideals, the things that you think highly of, the things you believe in.

The relationship between values and behavior is described in "The Cultural Equation," the brainchild of Dr. Garry A. Mendez, founder and executive director of the National Trust for the Development of African-American Men, a national nonprofit organization based in the Washington, D.C. area. Its premise is that one's behavior ought not be examined in a vacuum. Rather, all human behavior must be viewed in the context of values.

But how do we arrive at our values? As "The Cultural Equation" below illustrates, the starting point for all values, and thus behavior, is history. Even as individuals we all have a personal history, a narrative of past events. Our history plus culture (socially taught behavior) give us our values. In turn, our values produce our lifestyle, which is reflected in our behavior.

History	**+**	**Culture**	**=**	**Values**
Values	**→**	**Lifestyle**	**→**	**Behavior**

Birds Of a Feather

Friends…How many of us have them? Not many. When "Whoodini," the popular 1980s rap group, posed this question on one of their hit tracks, many people could relate. At the time I was in my early teens, too young to fully appreciate the question's significance. Like most teenagers, I wanted to fit in, to be accepted. I used the word *friend* loosely and regarded a bunch of people as friends.

The truth is that when you change your outlook on life, some of the people you once called friends will begin to look different. It'll seem as if they've transformed right before your eyes. But it's not them who've changed. It's *you*. Your perspective, the way you look at life (your future and the people in it) has broadened.

You'll know when your context has expanded, when you no longer think in narrow, limiting terms. How? Your so-called friends will gladly tell you so. They'll remind you that you're acting different, that you don't spend as much time with them as you once did: "You're always reading." "You're hanging out with those squares." "You talk differently."

Your so-called friends will tell you these things out of fear. They're afraid that you'll move on, that you'll grow and leave them behind. Like the proverbial crabs in a barrel, they will do everything in their power to pull you back down. They want you to stay in *your* place. Stay down and behind in life — with them.

Resist the urge to be loyal to "friends" who are going nowhere fast. Resist it with every ounce of strength and courage that you can muster. You'll be glad you did.

Michael Baisden, a syndicated radio talk-show host, says it best: "There are no neutral people." By that he means that people — in general and in your circle — either energize, motivate and bring out the best in you, or they drain your energy, stress you out and bring out the worst in you. The reality is that we call some of these energy drainers friends. And some are loved ones. Whatever, you need to assess and re-evaluate every person you deal with on a regular basis.

No doubt about it, some of them are holding you back from realizing your fullest potential. They may not be intentionally keeping you stagnant. (Then again, maybe they are.) But in the end it doesn't matter. You have to rid yourself of dead weight, rid yourself of baggage from your past, when you thought and behaved differently.

Your friends should reflect your new outlook on life, your expanded context. Birds of a feather *do* flock together. Drug dealers hang out with other drug dealers. Burglars associate with burglars. Robbers fraternize with other robbers.

Similarly, entrepreneurs *network* with other entrepreneurs. They create, build and change the world.

chapter 2

THINK BIG...START SMALL

NO MATTER YOUR CIRCUMSTANCES, one thing that cannot be taken away from you is your ability to dream big dreams, think big thoughts. This innate ability is your gift from the Creator. What you do with it will be the Creator's gift from you.

Thinking big means setting high goals for yourself. It means reaching for the stars, aiming high, dreaming the seemingly impossible. You will not accomplish big things unless you think big thoughts.

The reason most people do not think big is because they allow fear of failure or fear of success to get in the way. They listen to the small-minded talk of loved ones and so-called friends who tell them that their big dreams are just that — dreams. And they buy into their own negative self-talk that tells them that they're crazy for having such lofty dreams, that they ought to continue focusing on small, simple stuff.

Too often we play it small. We sell ourselves short. We believe negative stereotypes that are hurled at us. Stereotypes such as blacks are lazy, Latinos are stupid, or incarcerated people are incapable of changing for the better. These notions are all BS. But, unfortunately, some of us have bought into them.

You are bigger than the crime(s) you committed. Believe that! Your felony conviction(s) depicts your past. It says nothing about who you are today or what your future will entail! That's all up to you! By visualizing success, putting in hard work and never giving up, you *will* realize your dreams. No ifs ands or buts about it.

By nature, an entrepreneur thinks big. He pushes the envelope. In fact, entrepreneurs create the envelope. They don't fear change; they embrace it. For without change, entrepreneurs realize that they cannot grow as a person or grow their business.

The word "entrepreneur" comes from the French word *entreprendre*, which simply means risk taker, or to undertake. More to the point, an entrepreneur organizes and manages a business with the intention of making a profit while risking monetary loss.

There are two fundamental schools of thought when it comes to entrepreneurial ability. One school basically says that entrepreneurs are born, that you either have what it takes or you don't. The other school says that people can learn entrepreneurial skills, that even if you don't generally demonstrate a knack for business you can still become a successful entrepreneur.

Personally, I believe that anyone can become an entrepreneur. Notice I said *can*, not will. Just because someone has the ability to be successful in business doesn't mean he will assume the risk. Many of us already have some of the skills and characteristics necessary to do well in business. I believe that whatever we don't know, we can learn. I don't embrace the "either you have it or you don't" school of thought. There are countless examples of people who did not plan to go into business, but did so for various reasons. Some saw a need (or want) in the market that was not being met. Others lost their jobs, got divorced, retired, or were motivated by other considerations.

Ironically, incarcerated persons often develop and exhibit many entrepreneurial traits. The tough, competitive environments in which you've survived have also groomed you for business. While reading the characteristics of a successful entrepreneur below, reflect on your own aptitudes, your own dominant traits.

These twelve characteristics have been adopted, with permission, from Joseph Mancuso, best-selling author of "How to Get a Business Loan Without Signing Your life Away," and several other books. (Mancuso is also the founder of the Center for Entrepreneurial Management.) The list is by no means exhaustive. These are just some of the fundamental traits.

12 CHARACTERISTICS OF A SUCCESSFUL ENTREPRENEUR

1. Adaptability
2. Competitiveness
3. Confidence
4. Drive
5. Honesty
6. Organization
7. Persuasiveness
8. Discipline
9. Perseverance
10. Risk-taking
11. Understanding
12. Vision

Study each of the following entrepreneurial characteristics, keeping in mind that no one has all of them down pat.

Adaptability is the capacity to adjust to change, to roll with the punches. It means that *you* make changes — in your attitude, behavior and game plan — to deal with change. People with this characteristic don't become paralyzed when things don't go their way. Like the character Haw in Spencer Johnson's "Who Moved My Cheese?" they try to change or adapt to their circumstances because they know the alternative is to wallow in misery and self-pity. Or worse, they'll die.

Used wisely, the capacity to adjust to change will help you to overcome life's inevitable obstacles. In the process you will grow as a person and go far in life.

Competitiveness is a desire to compete, to test your skills and talents against others. This is another one of those traits that seem to be nurtured in young men and women who live in tough inner-city neighborhoods. Whether in the form of rapping (battling), playing the dozens or participating in sports, many of us have developed competitive personalities. Even when it comes down to the clothes and jewelry we wear or the vehicles we drive, being competitive runs deep in our bones. No doubt, this quality will serve you well in the world of business.

Confidence means believing in yourself and your ability to accomplish what you set out to do. Without confidence not much will be achieved. You can think big all you want, but if you don't believe in yourself, if you don't believe that you have what it takes to accomplish your goals, then you will not get very far in life.

The competitive spirit talked about earlier builds confidence in many of us. By testing our abilities and occasionally "winning," we learn to believe in our capabilities. The problem is that some of us become overconfident; we suffer delusions of grandeur, believing that we are more capable in certain things than we really are. We think we don't need others. That we can do everything on our own. The truth is we all need a helping hand. And in order for you to succeed, you must bring others along for the ride.

Confidence is as essential in life as it is in business. Just remember to stay humble. Don't let your skills, talents or success go to your head. Life is funny: one minute you might be on top of the world, and the next you could find yourself on the very bottom.

Drive is the motivation and burning desire to achieve your goals. It means not giving up when the going gets tough.

Like confidence and competitiveness, drive needs to be channeled properly. Otherwise, you'll do more harm than good to yourself and others.

Honesty means telling the truth, being sincere with others. Unlike most of the other entrepreneurial traits, honesty (or keeping it real —with yourself and others) is not something that necessarily comes easily for some of us.

Many of us learned to lie to avoid getting a whipping; we lied about our grades in school, about how much our parents made or what they did for a living. And we lied to avoid arrest and conviction.

No doubt our habit of being dishonest helped us get out of some scary situations. But being dishonest will hurt you in business and in life. One way or another it'll come back to haunt you. All you have to do is think of Enron to realize that lies and deception are not good for business. Once a model of American-style corporate success, it was forced into the largest bankruptcy in U.S. history for accounting violations, insider trading and securities fraud. Having integrity and being honest is always the way to go.

Organization is the ability to structure your life in efficient and effective ways. It means being able to keep tasks and information in order.

For too many of us, our childhood was anything but organized. This is another one of those traits that does not come easily. Unless you developed a facility for organization you will have to work on this important skill.

Persuasiveness is having the ability to convince others to see things as you do or to do something that you want them to do (or stop doing). It can involve having the gift of gab.

Discipline implies that you can stay focused, that you can stick to goals, objectives and agendas. Having discipline means that you don't allow people or things to take you off a course you've set upon.

Discipline was one of the hardest things for me to develop. I used to jump from one idea to another and spread myself thin, trying to accomplish too much without focusing and thinking things through, and without pacing myself. I assumed that by staying busy I was being productive. Not so.

About a year-and-a-half ago my wife, Sheila, talked me into giving myself permission to take time out every now and then. Without feeling guilty about it. (Yes, it was that bad.) She told me that I should keep the number of tasks on my plate manageable. That I could actually be *more* productive this way. At first the Aries in me resisted her logic. I was used to juggling a bunch of things at once. Used to moving from one task to the next without a breather. Often I would feel burned out but the habit of operating nonstop was difficult to break.

With nothing to lose, I began consciously fighting the urge—to pick up a book, write a letter, embark on a business plan. It wasn't easy, but it felt good each time I stopped in my tracks. And I felt liberated. Truly liberated.

For years I'd been a slave to my sense of urgency, a slave to my need to always feel productive and proficient. Truth be told, I still am busy working on one project or another on most days. But I *do* allow myself sufficient down time. And I no longer fight the occasional slacker in me. In the end I *am* more productive. I *am* more disciplined. Honestly, I owe it to my caring wife, who's my best friend and life partner.

Perseverance means not giving up on your goal. It means going the distance, even in the face of obstacles and temporary setbacks. For some of us, sticking it out comes easy. In fact, some of us have a single-minded determination to realize goals we have for ourselves. Others get weak in the knees as soon as things don't go their way. Which type of person are you?

Things will not always go your way. It's a fact of life. This is not the time to call it quits. Learn from every experience, and persevere. Even more, go the extra mile.

Risk-taking means putting yourself out there, exposing yourself to potential losses. In business, as in life, taking calculated risks can be a good thing. Often the greater the risk we take, the greater the potential reward. Being afraid to take risks could cost you money, business opportunities and rich learning experiences.

Sadly, many of us put our lives and loved ones' lives in jeopardy, without giving it much thought. We take risk-taking to a whole new level. The mindless risk-taking many of us are familiar with (because we been there, done that) lead countless people to prison. Some end up shot or stabbed. Others lose their lives. The risk-taking I'm touting is the healthy kind. The kind that is aimed at positive goals and is well thought out.

Understanding suggests that you not only listen to people but that you can put yourself in their shoes. In short, you can relate to people because you are able to see things as they do, you can feel what they're feeling. You can empathize.

Since you cannot have a business without customers, it is critical that you be able to understand how your customers think and what motivates them.

More often than not many of us cling to an unhealthy and stifling victim mentality. This gets in the way of our being able to see beyond our own painful experiences, our own jaded thoughts.

In business it's not about you. It's about your customers. Learn to understand and appreciate them, and they will reward you.

Vision is having the ability to imagine yourself accomplishing your goals. It's being able to envision yourself having what you want, living the lifestyle you desire and being surrounded by the people you want to be amongst. Vision is a mental activity. It's half of the equation. The other half is physical. It requires you to do whatever it takes to reach your goals, whatever it takes to accomplish your dreams.

It is said that everything happens twice, first internally (in your head), then externally (in the physical world). Having vision is the first step toward becoming a successful entrepreneur.

PLAYING THE PART

Keep it real: how many of the above-mentioned traits do you have? One? Three? Five? Which ones do you need to work on? Remember, no one has all of the traits of an entrepreneur. As long as you have several of them under your belt you can rely on your team members (or business partners) for the others. Or try to develop the areas where you're lacking.

You are what you consistently think about, and what you consistently do. If you really want to be a successful entrepreneur you have to read business books, magazines and the business section of newspapers in order to stay abreast of what's happening in the business world and, just as important, to develop a knack for recognizing business opportunities. This is key. In the process, you'll discover all sorts of business opportunities.

Do as other entrepreneurs do: study other successful entrepreneurs. Stay on top of business and economic and political news. And always look for hidden business opportunities.

GET WITH THE PROGRAM

Tennis legend Arthur Ashe once said "Start where you are, use what you have, do what you can." The essence of Ashe's wise words signifies what this chapter is about: applying and improving upon skills and aptitudes you already have to achieve your goals.

PRISON AS YOUR TRAINING GROUND

Prison is no walk in the park. That's for sure. Prison life can be tough, dangerous and then some. At the same time, prison *can* be an educationally rewarding experience. No, I'm not talking about college programs. (Unfortunately, Congress did away with extending the Pell Grant for incarcerated persons in 1994. And the vast majority of states followed suit.) I'm talking about identifying your strengths and weaknesses, focusing on the things you are passionate about and honing skills that will make you a better person and entrepreneur. Rather than allowing prison to weigh you down, make it your teacher. To live is to learn — no matter where you happen to be.

Make prison your training ground in the same way that some people work for a company in a field that they intend to start a business in, so that they can get hands-on experience and learn the lay of the land in order to start their own business.

Take full advantage of prison programs. Don't make the mistake of discounting all the skills that you've learned while in prison. Skills like carpentry, plumbing, computer diagnostics and repair, cooking and horticulture, to name a few. If you have any of these skills, chances are you can turn them into a business someday. For instance, if you love to cook, you might want to consider opening a restaurant or starting a catering business. If you have a knack for fixing computers you can either open up a computer repair shop (perhaps home-based) or start a computer consulting business. Other businesses, government agencies and individuals are always in need of people with computer skills.

The point is use whatever skills and talents you have to build a business around. Maybe you don't have the "hard" skills mentioned above. Perhaps you're more like me in that you're not good with your hands. Instead, you like to exercise your mind in thinking critically, in analyzing things. For instance, you may have "soft" skills like legal research, public speaking or organizational skills. These, too, can be turned into businesses.

Rather than waste your time and energy on things you don't enjoy doing, on things you have no intention of pursuing when you are paroled, focus your efforts on things that will either directly or indirectly tie into your business aspirations. Do what you love and love what you do.

It's bad enough you're in prison. Don't make matters worse by wasting your time!

Even though I began this chapter talking about starting where you are (in prison or recently paroled) I would be negligent if I did not remind you that when you came to prison you already possessed a range of skills. It doesn't matter that you grew up in a rough neighborhood, or that you dropped out of school. At home you may have acquired people skills, cooking skills or negotiation skills. Likewise, on the streets many of you probably developed organizational, analytical, marketing and sales skills and the ability to make quick, decisive decisions. These are all valuable skills to bring to any business.

Reflect for a few minutes on skills and talents that you currently have, skills that you might be taking for granted. Skills that could possibly serve as the foundation for a business. You'll be surprised at what you can already do.

ASSESSING YOUR STRENGTHS AND WEAKNESSES

It's not enough to know what you're good at. Just as you have a number of strengths in your favor, you no doubt have weaknesses, some of which are probably hindering you from getting ahead.

Before investing a great deal of time and energy into planning to start a business, you should do an honest assessment of your strengths *and* your weaknesses. A personal inventory.

While some of your weaknesses can be minimized or eliminated altogether, you'd be better off focusing on building on your strengths. That is, you should play to your strengths, what you're really good at.

Don't misconstrue this to mean that you should overlook your weaknesses. That would be a big mistake.

TIME MANAGEMENT

Time is like money: if you invest it wisely you're likely to reap a handsome dividend. But if there is no investment, guess what? There's no "return" on investment.

We all have twenty-four hours in a day to make use of. It doesn't matter if you're rich, poor, black, white, free or incarcerated. As far as hours in a day go, we're on an even playing field. What distinguishes us is *how* we invest our time. And how we invest our time is a reflection of our values.

Quite often what we say we value and how we spend our time are not in alignment with each other. We say one thing and do another. For example, we all know people who say they value freedom, that they have a burning desire to go home to their loved ones. Yet these are some of the same people who not only don't hit the books in the law library, they're the ones who spend most of their time playing ball on the basketball court, pumping iron or mindlessly watching TV.

This doesn't mean that they don't want to go home. Of course they do. But their priorities are not in order. In the end, it's not what we say but what we do that matters.

A starting point on getting a handle on how you currently *invest* your time is for you to fill out the time management chart below. Write in the activity you most often do during the time slots. Then once you've completed the chart, decide whether you're wisely investing your time. If not, devise a plan that will make better use of it.

I'm not suggesting that you'll be able to change on a dime. Old habits are hard to break. But decide right now that you will invest your time and live your life in ways that reflect your true values and life goals.

Hours	Monday	Tuesday	Wednesday	Thursday	Friday	Saturday	Sunday
7 — 8 am							
8 — 9 am							
9 — 10 am							
10 — 11 am							
11 — Noon							
Noon — 1 pm							
1 — 2 pm							
2 — 3 pm							

3 — 4 pm							
4 — 5 pm							
5 — 6 pm							
6 — 7 pm							
7 — 8 pm			.				
8 — 9 pm							
9 — 10 pm							
10 — 11 pm							

I bet you were surprised by what you learned about yourself from the chart. That's normal. So what to do? Make a commitment to yourself — right now — to invest a minimum of one hour every day in doing something that advances you to realizing your business goals. It could be as simple as reading the business section of the newspaper, listening to a self-help or business cassette, watching CNBC. Or listening to business — or investment-oriented — radio programs.

Whatever, the important thing is to remain focused on your plan. Do not take your eyes off the prize.

What, you're too busy to set aside one hour *every* day? Well, you had better become less busy. This is *your* life we're talking about. *Your* future. *Your* freedom.

Just one hour a day turns into seven hours a week, thirty hours a month, 365 hours a year. Talk about investing your time…Talk about return on investment.

SETTING GOALS

Having goals will give you a sense of purpose, a sense of direction. It will help you to focus your attention, time and energy on things you set out to accomplish.

Without goals you'll walk around aimlessly. You'll be easily swayed by others' intentions, others' ideas about what's best for you. That's not what this book is about.

The fact that you are reading this book suggests that one of your goals is to start your own business. That's all good, but have you given much thought to *how* you intend to make your goals a reality? Have you seriously thought about the step-by-step process required for you to own your own business?

Too often we set lofty goals without considering *how* we will achieve them. We see ourselves with the fancy car and nice house, but we don't take time out to figure out the steps to get them. The truth is, goals come a dime a dozen. The real work is in taking the time out (the days, weeks and months) to put together a well-thought-out plan. The real work is in putting one foot in front of the other and living our goals.

Until you've committed your goals to writing they will remain a dream. Writing down your goals makes them real. And it makes you committed to your goals.

Everything you do should serve a purpose. How you invest your time. What you eat. What you read. Even when it comes to down time (we *do* need balance in our lives), you need to be clear that that's what it is: down time. An opportunity to rest, to rejuvenate your mind, body and soul. Being clear about this reduces the likelihood that you'll mistake down time for those times when you're supposed to actively be working toward a goal.

SMART

Let's take a practical approach to laying out your goal of starting a business when you get out of prison. What might your goal-setting outline look like? What will you have to do? Who will you go to for help? How much research and start-up capital will you need? How long will it take? (Chapters 7 and 8 go into greater detail about writing a business plan and running your business.)

The SMART acronym stands for **S**pecific, **M**easurable, **A**ction-oriented, **R**ealistic and **T**imely.

Be <u>Specific</u>. In this case, your goal might be to start, say, a mail-order catalog that caters to incarcerated men and women. If you had only said you intend to start a business, that would not have been specific enough. To be specific you'd have to be clear about what type of business you plan to start and who your target market is. You could be even more specific by stating that your company will sell to state prisons (as opposed to federal) and that your aim is to target people in the southeastern region of the country. How specific you are when writing down your goals is up to you. But you need to be specific.

Now that you've spelled out your business goals, how will you know if you're on track to reaching them? You do it by setting benchmarks, <u>Measurable</u> yardsticks that indicate where you're at in terms of your goals. These benchmarks will tell you how close you are to reaching your ultimate goals. I say ultimate because you should have mini-goals along the way to reaching your major goal: starting your mail-order business.

For example, some of your mini-goals might be to write a sound business plan in three months, form an advisory board in six months and register your business in one year.

Talk is cheap. In order for you to realize your goal of starting a business you'll need to put in the necessary work. Fantasizing about running your own business, about being your own boss, won't make it a reality. Your goals must be <u>**Action-oriented**</u>. They must spell out exactly what you intend to do to attain them. Without action your goals will be relegated to a dream world.

What steps will you take to get your business off the ground? For starters, you will certainly need to read books and magazines about how to start and run a mail-order business. You'll want to collect and study the catalogs of businesses that already sell to incarcerated men and women. These companies will become your direct competitors. Also, you'll want to write relevant trade associations for up-to-date stats and information about the size of and trends of players in the mail-order industry.

Why do you want to start a business? Why a mail-order business that caters to incarcerated persons? Do you have the financial means to start the business? If not, will you be able to secure a loan from family members or friends? What about getting a bank loan? Are you even passionate about business? Or does your motivation come from the fact that everyone and their mama (even correctional staff) have started mail-order businesses catering to men and women in prison, so you figure why not jump on the bandwagon?

I'm not trying to discourage you from going into business. That would defeat the purpose of this book. The point I'm trying to make is that you need to be <u>Realistic</u> about your goals. Think them through. And do an inventory of your strengths and weaknesses, and your motivations. Also, think in terms of the resources you have and the resources you'll need to start your business. Besides money, you will need human resources (people) and time.

Some business opportunities have a small window of opportunity. By this I mean if you do not act quickly, others may beat you to the punch by starting a similar business and gaining a considerable share of the market. An example of a window of opportunity would be trying to sell books or posters based on a popular movie. Chances are once the movie is no longer at the box office, once it is no longer a part of everyday conversations, it will no longer be <u>Timely</u> for you to be in such a business or to be selling those particular books and posters. (There are exceptions, of course.)

Business ideas may pop into your head several times a day. But business *opportunities* are something different. Business opportunities are based on what customers want. They're based on having an existing window of opportunity, having the resources and skills to take advantage of the opportunity and making sure the opportunity is suitable for your business environment. Timeliness is a crucial factor that must be considered when planning to embark on a business opportunity.

chapter 3

ABOUT THEM BENJAMINS

WHAT GOOD IS IT to make lots of money if you can't manage it? If you can't keep it long enough to put it to good use?

Many of us have a hustle mentality. We have a gift of gab and know how to make a dollar out of fifteen cents. When we were home we wore the latest fashions, leased or owned the nicest cars, trucks and motor bikes, and we took trips to exotic locales. But what did we have to show for all of this styling and profiling when we got arrested? Nothing!

Granted, some people bought homes, savings bonds for their children's educations and made other wise investments. But keep it real: most of us didn't even have enough money to retain a good attorney when we got arrested. We scrambled to try to get money for a lawyer from family members and so-called friends.

In this country owning your own home, your own business or stocks and bonds is what counts. But when we got arrested there was no home, business or stocks and bonds to put up as collateral for bail. And our lawyers had no use for our designer clothes or jewelry. They had no use for our leased cars. They wanted money.

The painful truth is we just hadn't *planned* to get arrested. That's right, planned. Even worse, we left dependents behind to fend for themselves: our children, our wives and girlfriends, our husbands and boyfriends, and our siblings.

Unfortunately, too many of us acted like committing crimes was our job. There was no exit strategy. Instead we continued on with our madness, essentially living for the moment. So when we did get arrested we were caught totally off guard. Without a plan. And with nothing to show for all the mayhem we had created. To be sure, saving and investing were the furthest things from our minds.

Surviving by any means necessary came natural to us. We didn't grow up having dinner-table discussions with our parents about such things as saving, budgeting, banking or investing. Those topics were not a priority, given the myriad pressing issues that often overwhelmed our families. Our parents just didn't have the time — or skills — to teach us how money works.

You would think that in the most capitalistic nation in the world financial literacy would be taught as early as first grade, right alongside reading, writing and arithmetic. Unfortunately, financial literacy and basic business and economic principles are not taught in our public school systems. One has to take courses on these topics in college. Or learn them the hard way by dealing with banks or investment brokers.

The fact that most people are *illiterate* and lack discipline when it comes to basic things such as how to write a check or how the stock market works partly explains the skyrocketing credit card debt and personal and business bankruptcies in this country. It also explains why it's not uncommon for some drug dealers or robbers to purchase $40,000 and $50,000 automobiles — even though they still live in the projects. That same $50,000, if invested as a down payment for a home, would likely appreciate or go up in value. The value of the car or truck, on the other hand, will depreciate the moment it's driven off the lot. By as much as twenty percent. In this case, that would amount to an $8,000 to $10,000 loss, from the jump. That's not a smart move, but because we weren't equipped with even a fundamental sense of the value of money and how money works, many of us consistently made poor decisions with our money. In the end, we wind up paying a high price for our illiteracy.

When I got arrested in March 1992, I had less than $3,000 stashed away. I did not own a home. Nor did I own a business or stocks and bonds. In fact I knew very little about how to purchase a home. I'd considered starting a business but didn't know the first step to take. And, to tell you the truth, I thought owning stocks and bonds was for other people. Not me. I thought I had to be rich in order to invest in stocks and bonds. I was clueless when it came to all of this stuff.

In the beginning months of my prison term I maintained a relatively carefree lifestyle. I wore mostly designer shirts and sweaters (pants other than state-issued are not allowed), and expensive sneakers and boots. Each time I "shopped" during bi-monthly commissary buy dates I spent close to the maximum permitted. When guys in the yard pitched greeting cards they'd drawn and other handmade wares, I bought them without giving it a second thought.

One day an old-timer, a friend of a friend, questioned me about my spending habits. "Why do you waste your money on junk? You make decent money in the plate-making shop, but I notice you spend a lot in commissary. You should save your money, youngblood."

"Listen, bro," I said. "I'll spend *my* money however *I* want. I don't need you telling me how to spend my money." I stared him down.

"You're right. You're right." He smiled and walked away mumbling.

Five months later I was transferred to Elmira Correctional Facility to begin serving time for the murder conviction. I was slapped with a hefty $155 court-ordered surcharge. At the time I had $92 in my prison inmate account, money I'd brought with me from my previous facility.

Since Elmira was a reception center, I was only allowed to keep my legal documents, my mail and a bible. I had to send the rest of my personal property home, including my toiletries.

The $92 that I'd managed to save was promptly withdrawn from my account to pay for the court-ordered surcharge. That wasn't the end of it; half of any money that I received from the outside and twenty percent of prison earnings would be deducted from my account until the surcharge was fully paid.

The surcharge might as well have been a million dollars. I felt like the victim of a robbery, of state-sanctioned extortion.

For the next month or so, I didn't have enough money to even buy myself a bar of soap, a stick of deodorant or a tube of toothpaste. I was at the mercy of the Department of Corrections. They would supply me with lye-based soap and gummy toothpaste. They didn't issue deodorant, so I had to be careful not to work up too much of a sweat.

Fortunately, I befriended a few guys whose generosity and compassion helped me get through that tough period.

With the financial help of longtime friends Mark and Jan Folsom, I eventually satisfied the surcharge. But the experience was a humbling one. From that point on I vowed to never again be careless with my money. I vowed to value money and learn how to use it wisely.

Face it: on your parole date, your loved ones won't be waiting for you outside the gates of prison with a duffel bag full of money. That's just not reality. Sure, they love you and want to support your successful transition back to the community, but most of them are struggling to make ends meet. Most of them are living from paycheck to paycheck.

While certainly a strain on their modest budgets, it is less expensive for your loved ones to send you food and care packages, to buy you sneakers and sweat suits while you are *in* prison. When you go home all of that will change. No longer will they be able to support you in the way that they tried to do while you were incarcerated. The money just isn't there.

That's why it's crucial that you begin saving money while you're still in prison. Don't waste the money that you earn from prison assignments. I know, prison "wages" are meager. (And that's putting it mildly.) But you still need to develop good spending and budgeting habits so that you don't go home with your hands held out. So you don't go home feeling like your back is against the wall. Feeling like you *have* to rob, steal or sell drugs in order to make a living. You don't.

Another reason you should begin saving while in prison is because the chances of your getting a small business loan (especially with a felony conviction) are extremely slim. Even if you have a great business idea. In fact, more than half the people who start businesses do so with money from their personal savings, credit cards and loans from family members and friends. Since your loved ones are probably having a hard time making ends meet and you don't own credit cards, that leaves *your* personal savings.

So where to begin?

Money Power: An 8-Step Plan for Incarcerated Persons

As with most things in life, you need to have a plan for not only becoming financially literate but for parlaying money for when you get out of prison.

The following 8-step plan will set you on the right track.

Step 1: Assess Your Values

Before you do anything else take a critical look at the things that reflect your values: the people, issues, goals and passions that are most important to you. Remember, your values and beliefs determine your behavior.

Ask yourself: *If I had only one month to live (and enough money to do as I pleased) how would I spend my time? What activities would I partake in? Who would I want to be surrounded by? Where would I travel? What projects or ventures would I get involved in?*

You get the idea.

Right now take out a blank piece of paper. Write down the top ten things that you value most. Then write them down again, this time in the order of importance to you. Don't rush. Think this stuff through. Now write down one or two goals for each of the prioritized values. These can be short-term or long-term or both.

Finally, write down the steps you intend to take to realize your goals, to demonstrate your values. For example, let's say you wrote down "family" as your number one value. You can't just say that you value family. You have to show it. You have to live your values. In this case, one of your goals might be to show family members you love them and a step could be to write a loved one a letter — or poem — expressing your love, appreciation or concern.

Keep in mind, your values and priorities will change from time to time. As a result, the goals you set should reflect these changes.

Step 2: Determine Your Short- and Long-Term Goals

This step focuses specifically on your financial goals. It involves the careful planning of what you want to accomplish over the short term and long term with respect to wealth accumulation. You should be very specific: In six months I will open a savings account with $300; I will invest $1,000 in an aggressive growth fund in five years.

Step 3: Gather And Organize Your Financial Records

In business the most common financial statements are balance sheet, profit and loss statement (also called income statement) and cash-flow statement. Together these statements paint a picture of the financial health of a business. Similarly, your prison financial records reveal not only your spending and saving habits, but also your personal financial health. Bear in mind, your habits reflect your values.

Begin collecting your financial records so that you can better track your spending patterns. Do it now. Take out any financial records that you've stored away. (Receipts, invoices, etc.) You know, the ones that have collected dust. Separate them by category (monthly statements, receipts, etc.), placing each in their own pile. Review them. They tell a story all their own.

Step 4: Distinguish Between Your Wants And Needs

O.K., you've separated and organized your financial records. It's time to take a closer look at what they say about you. Take out a blank piece of paper. Draw a line down the center. At the top left write the word *Needs*. At the top right write *Wants*.

Using any of your commissary receipts or monthly statements, write down each item or financial transaction under the column where it rightly belongs. Be honest with yourself.

Do you *need* cigarettes? Do you *need* coffee and junk food? All too often we become so accustomed to buying certain things that we convince ourselves that we actually need them. The truth is, as this exercise shows, we *need* a lot less than we think.

So what have you learned about your spending habits from this exercise? I bet the list was lopsided, with a laundry list of wants and a comparatively smaller list of needs. From now on think about whether something you intend to buy is a want or a need. If it's a want and you feel comfortable making the purchase, then go right ahead. But if you don't feel comfortable, put your money to better use.

Blurring the lines between wants and needs is not unique to incarcerated persons. People on the outside also have trouble distinguishing between the two. They too confuse their wants with their needs.

I'm in no way suggesting that you deprive yourself of nice things, that you not indulge yourself every now and then. But don't go overboard. Not if you're serious about achieving your goal of someday starting a business.

Step 5: Create A Realistic Budget

Planning and sticking to a budget will hold you accountable. Not any budget, though. Yours must take into consideration the financial goals (what you are trying to accomplish) you've set. It has to also factor in your current lifestyle. By this I mean how you spend your money and time.

Since you'll be paying closer attention to your spending habits, it will be easier to realize your goals. This is because by regularly going over weekly, monthly and yearly budgets you will in effect be reinforcing your commitment to your goals.

Your budget should include the sources and amounts of income received from loved ones, friends and prison jobs. It should also contain a record of your expenses. These may consist of court-mandated restitution, surcharges, commissary purchases, the cost of disciplinary infractions (tickets), etc.

The idea is to focus on your financial needs first while satisfying your wants in moderation. Sticking to a realistic budget will help you do this, and achieve your short- and long-term financial goals.

Step 6: Get Educated

Your journey to financial literacy does not end with establishing a budget. In fact, it never ends!

Take full advantage of the books, magazines and other business or personal finance materials that your prison library has. Start with the basic stuff, then gradually take on more advanced topics.

The more you read, the more likely you are to come across bibliographies and other references to books, magazines and newsletters that interest you. Create a running list of these materials, and as you read them check them off.

Chances are your facility's library won't have all the books you're looking for. In that case, ask the librarian whether the library is part of an interlibrary loan (ILL) system. If so, find out how it works. Generally, when your library doesn't have a particular book you're interested in you can simply request the book from the network of libraries that participate in interlibrary loans. It won't cost you a dime since you'd still be *borrowing* books.

What if your facility isn't part of such a system. Ask the librarian or prison administrators how your facility can participate in one. If no library exists within your facility, get together with your peers and ask them to individually request that a library be added to the facility's budget. In the meantime borrow books from your peers.

Step 7: Establish A Personal Library

If you have the means, create your own personal library. Subscribe to business and personal finance magazines and newsletters. Purchase books and audiotapes. (See Appendix B for a list of books, magazines and web sites that will get you started.) Another possibility is to pool together with a few peers to subscribe to a wider range of magazines and newsletters. This will save all of you money. At the same time, each of you will be able to read more publications than would otherwise be possible.

Step 8: Spread The Word

What good is enriching information if you can't share it with the people you care about most? As you flex your financial literacy muscles be sure to bring your peers and loved ones along with you for the ride.

As for your peers, try to form a small team of men (or women) who want to learn about personal finance or starting a business. Start a focus group or think tank. Eventually the group may want to draft a manual or course curriculum for a class or workshop to be offered to a large group of peers.

Keep the information simple and interesting and you'll no doubt have a captive audience. (No pun intended.)

When it comes to your loved ones, keep in mind that many of them have their eyes set on the here and now. They can't see six months ahead, let alone five or ten years down the road. And since financial literacy is not taught in your public schools (or even most private schools), learning this topic will be like learning a foreign language. You'll have to take it slow and constantly emphasize the benefits of saving and investing. (Chapter 4 goes more into how to bring your loved ones up to speed.)

SAVING & INVESTING

Though the words saving and investing are often used interchangeably, they are *not* the same thing. Here's why:

Saving can mean anything from stashing money under a mattress or in a safe-deposit box for safekeeping to putting it in a low-interest savings account at a bank. In either case your money isn't working hard enough for you. Putting money in a bank account is playing it safe.

Don't get me wrong; it's better to save than not. At least you'll have a cash reserve when you need it. But don't confuse saving with investing.

Say you stashed $25,000 in a safe-deposit box before you got arrested. You can't wait to get paroled so you can get your hands on that money. Now, let's suppose you've been in prison for seven years and have three years before your parole date. Guess what? The *value* of the $25,000 has diminished considerably. The money no longer has the purchasing power that it did when you stashed it. Sure, when you count the currency (if it hasn't already been "borrowed" by a loved one or so-called friend) you'll have $25,000. But that money won't buy you half as much as it once could. Its buying power has dwindled.

Inflation, or the general rise in price levels in the economy, is the culprit. Along with interest rates (another way of saying "the cost of borrowing money"), inflation has a corrosive effect on your money's purchasing power. This is important to remember when implementing any saving or investing strategy.

Investing involves putting your money to work, not just saving for a rainy day. The risk of losing money usually increases with investing, but so does the potential to increase the real value of your money. This is because, in theory, the riskier an investment is, the greater the *potential* is for higher earnings. Likewise, the less risky an investment is the less your gains are likely to be. Whether saving or investing, this risk-reward concept applies across the board.

One way to analyze savings and investment options is to compare interest rates earned. Of course you want the highest possible rates — without exposing yourself to too much risk. But how can you determine how much interest you're actually earning, or how long it will take for your money to double?

There are essentially two types of interest: simple interest and compound interest. The two tables below provide a glimpse of how your money grows much faster (exponentially) when earnings and interest are compounded.

A brief definition of the two types of interest:

Simple Interest is interest calculated on principal alone.

Compound Interest, simply put, is interest upon interest; that is, interest paid on principal *plus* accrued interest.

Let's now suppose that you opened two separate bank accounts, one earning simple interest, the other earning compound interest. You deposit $1,000 in each account, with both paying 10% interest. You leave the money in the bank for the next seven years. The main difference between the two accounts is *how* your interest is calculated.

Simple Interest

	Principal	Interest Rate	Interest Earned in $	Return on Investment
Year 1	$1,000	10%	$100	$1,100 ($1,000 + $100)
Year 2	$1,100	"	"	$1,200 ($1,100 + $100)
Year 3	$1,200	"	"	$1,300 ($1,200 + $100)
Year 4	$1,300	"	"	$1,400 ($1,300 + $100)
Year 5	$1,400	"	"	$1,500 ($1,400 + $100)
Year 6	$1,500	"	"	$1,600 ($1,500 + $100)

Year 7	$1,600	"	"	$1,700 ($1,600 + $100)

Compound Interest

	Principal	Interest Rate	Interest Earned in $	Return on Investment
Year 1	$1,000	10%	$100	$1,100 ($1,000 + $100)
Year 2	$1,100	"	$110	$1,210 ($1,100 + $110)
Year 3	$1,210	"	$121	$1,331 ($1,210 + $121)
Year 4	$1,331	"	$133.10	$1,464.10 ($1,331 + $133.10)
Year 5	$1,464.10	"	$146.41	$1,610.51 ($1,464.10 + $146.41)
Year 6	$1,610.51	"	$161.05	$1,771.51 ($1,610.51 + $161.05)
Year 7	$1,771.56	"	$177.15	$1,948.72 ($1,771.56 + $177.15)

At first glance, there may seem to be no marked difference between simple and compound interest. This is because it takes a little while for the full effect of compound interest to take hold.

Notice that at the end of Year 1 your returns on investment (another way of saying the money you made) in your bank account balances are identical: $1,100. But by Year 6 you start seeing a noticeable difference. The account earning compound interest begins to stand out. At the end of Year 7 it has just about doubled, while the simple interest account has only provided you with a $1,700 balance, a difference of almost $300.

The longer your money earns compound interest the more pronounced your gains will be. Using the "Rule of 72," you can calculate how long it will take for your money to double — over and over again.

The "Rule of 72" works like this: simply divide your return on investment (interest rate) into the number 72. For instance, using the compound interest chart above we saw that $1,000 invested at 10% a year became almost $2,000 (or double your original investment) at the end of seven years.

Here's the math:

$$72 \div 10 = 7.2 \text{ years} \quad \text{or} \quad 72/10 = 7.2 \text{ years}$$

At 10% interest your money will double every seven years. The higher the interest rate, the faster your money will compound — and double.

A few more examples:

$$72 \div 15 = 4.8 \text{ years} \quad \text{or} \quad 72/15 = 4.8 \text{ years}$$
$$72 \div 8 = 9 \text{ years} \quad \text{or} \quad 72/8 = 9 \text{ years}$$
$$72 \div 12 = 6 \text{ years} \quad \text{or} \quad 72/12 = 6 \text{ years}$$

By consistently adding money to your investments your total return will grow even faster. Take a look at the following three tables to see what I mean.

8% Average Annual Return

Monthly Investment

	1 Year	5 Years	10 Years	15 Years	20 Years	25 Years	30 Years
$ 200	$ 2,503	$ 14,683	$ 36,527	$ 67,957	$114,534	$182,973	$ 283,532
$ 300	$ 3,754	$ 22,024	$ 54,385	$101,935	$171,802	$274,459	$ 425,298
$ 400	$ 5,006	$ 29,366	$ 72,514	$135,913	$229,069	$365,945	$ 567,064
$ 500	$ 6,257	$ 36,707	$ 90,642	$169,892	$286,336	$457,432	$ 708,830
$ 600	$ 7,508	$ 44,049	$108,771	$203,870	$343,603	$548,918	$ 850,596
$ 700	$ 8,760	$ 51,390	$126,899	$237,848	$400,870	$640,405	$ 992,362
$ 800	$ 10,011	$ 58,731	$145,028	$271,827	$458,137	$731,891	$1,134,128
$ 900	$ 11,263	$ 66,073	$163,156	$305,805	$515,405	$823,377	$1,275,894
$ 1,000	$ 12,514	$ 73,414	$181,285	$339,783	$572,672	$914,864	$1,417,660

10% Average Annual Return

Monthly Investment

	1 Year	5 Years	10 Years	15 Years	20 Years	25 Years	30 Years
$ 200	$ 2,528	$ 15,434	$ 40,292	$ 80,324	$ 144,797	$ 248,632	$ 415,859
$ 300	$ 3,792	$ 23,152	$ 60,437	$ 120,486	$ 217,196	$ 372,948	$ 623,788
$ 400	$ 5,056	$ 30,869	$ 80,583	$ 160,649	$ 289,595	$ 497,264	$ 831,717
$ 500	$ 6,320	$ 38,586	$ 100,729	$ 200,811	$ 361,993	$ 621,580	$1,039,647
$ 600	$ 7,584	$ 46,303	$ 120,875	$ 240,973	$ 434,392	$ 745,896	$1,247,576
$ 700	$ 8,848	$ 54,020	$ 141,020	$ 281,135	$ 506,791	$ 870,212	$1,455,505
$ 800	$ 10,112	$ 61,737	$ 161,166	$ 321,297	$ 579,189	$ 994,528	$1,663,435
$ 900	$ 11,376	$ 69,455	$ 181,312	$ 361,459	$ 651,588	$1,118,844	$1,871,364
$ 1,000	$ 12,641	$ 77,172	$ 201,458	$ 401,621	$ 723,987	$1,243,160	$2,079,293

12% Average Annual Return

Monthly Investment

	1 Year	5 Years	10 Years	15 Years	20 Years	25 Years	30 Years
$ 200	$ 2,553	$ 16,221	$ 44,807	$ 95,186	$ 183,972	$ 340,442	$ 616,196
$ 300	$ 3,830	$ 24,331	$ 67,211	$ 142,780	$ 275,958	$ 510,663	$ 924,294
$ 400	$ 5,107	$ 32,441	$ 89,614	$ 190,373	$ 367,943	$ 680,884	$1,232,392
$ 500	$ 6,383	$ 40,552	$ 112,018	$ 237,966	$ 459,929	$ 851,105	$1,540,489
$ 600	$ 7,660	$ 48,662	$ 134,422	$ 285,559	$ 551,915	$1,021,325	$1,848,587
$ 700	$ 8,937	$ 56,773	$ 145,825	$ 333,152	$ 643,901	$1,191,546	$2,156,685
$ 800	$ 10,213	$ 64,883	$ 179,229	$ 380,745	$ 735,887	$1,361,767	$2,464,783
$ 900	$ 11,490	$ 72,993	$ 201,632	$ 428,339	$ 827,873	$1,531,988	$2,772,881
$ 1,000	$ 12,766	$ 81,104	$ 224,036	$ 475,932	$ 919,858	$1,702,209	$3,080,979

Before charging full speed ahead on your saving or investing journey, check with your facilities law library or prison administrators about any rules, policies or procedures that may prohibit incarcerated persons from opening bank accounts or investing in stocks, bonds or mutual funds. If your facility has such a policy, don't get discouraged. Although it won't be the same as having a bank account (or investments) in your own name, Plan B is to choose a loved one or friend who'd be willing to put your money to work for you.

The downside to this approach is that the account will probably be in *their* name, not yours. Make sure you trust this person! Money has a tendency to bring out the worst in some people. (The next chapter talks about how you can get others to help you attain your financial and business goals.)

People say to me all the time: "I have x amount of money saved. What should I do with it? Where should I invest it?" The expression on their faces telegraphs their hope that I'll confide in them some hot stock tip, some clever way for them to flip their savings twofold or threefold in a matter of months. When I tell them that it's not that simple, that several things ought to be taken into consideration before deciding how best to put their money to work, I'm met with a puzzled look.

"O.K., what do I need to know?" they ask.

My immediate reply: "First, you need to know what your goals are. Your financial goals, and your life goals. You have to know where you're trying to go, what you are trying to accomplish."

"I'm trying to make money."

"I know that. But you need to be clear and specific about *why* you want to make money."

"*Why?*" they ask. I can tell that I've confused them. Either that or they think I'm crazy. But I continue.

"Yeah, why do you want to make money? What do you plan to do with it? Will it be for your child's education? A business? A down payment on a home?" By now I've really grabbed their attention. I've got them thinking. "That's the first thing you need to consider."

"What else?"

I smile at their antsy inquisitiveness. "Now you got the right idea."

I then ask them how old they are. My question is usually met with another puzzled look.

"Though it's never too late to begin saving or investing, the earlier you do so the better. This is because your money will have more time to grow. And with time on your side you won't have to worry as much about weathering financial storms like a down stock market or sluggish economy. You'll have more wiggle room than you would if you needed to get your hands on your money in, say, three or four years. So the sooner you put your money to work the better."

"Well, that's why I've come to you asking about where to invest my money."

"Right. But there are two other things you need to think about before jumping out there without a parachute."

"What is it?" they ask impatiently.

"How much risk are you willing to take with your money? Would you be willing to lose all or some of your money if you thought you could possibly earn a nice gain?"

"I'm not sure," they say. "I'm not into gambling. I hate losing money."

"Me, too. And this is why your tolerance for risk is another factor that comes into play when it comes to where to put your money."

"I see. That makes sense."

"Oh, and one more thing."

"What's that?" they eagerly ask.

"How *much* money you have available will determine *where* you can invest."

This type of conversation gets rehashed with little variation. Each time, the potential investor walks away a little more informed, and a little more prudent when it comes to investing.

SAVINGS ACCOUNT

Traditional savings accounts come in two flavors: passbook and transaction. With the passbook type you receive a stack of vouchers that allow you to deposit or withdraw money from your account. The vouchers resemble a book of blank checks. An example is on the following page.

Ordinarily if you wanted to deposit or withdraw money using this type of account, you could do so at a moment's notice. But the process will take a little longer since you'll be going through prison staff (most likely a counselor) to make all transactions. If a loved one opens an account for you, all you have to do is communicate your intentions to him or her.

You may want to avoid the record-keeping demands of a passbook savings account, which requires you to fill out and maintain a record of every transaction you've made over a given period of time. With the transaction account, the bank, savings and loan or credit union will do all of this for you. Each month they'll send you a computer-generated copy of all of the deposits and withdrawals that you made during the previous month. The statement will also show your current balance, the amount of interest you've earned and any fees incurred. Read your statements carefully. Bank personnel (and computers) *do* sometimes make mistakes. That's why it's a good idea for you to keep your own updated records. In this way you can balance your books, checking for any discrepancies.

```
┌─────────────────────────────────────────────────────────────────┐
│  SAVINGS ACCOUNT DEPOSIT SLIP                                     │
│                                                                   │
│  NAME_____                                      │
│                                   Date_____  20_____   │
│  ACCT. NO. _____                                      │
│                                                                   │
│                                              Dollars     Cents    │
│  ─────────────────────────────    Currency  │         │        │ │
│        For Classroom Use Only     Coin      │         │        │ │
│  ALL ITEMS ARE ACCEPTED SUBJECT   Checks    │         │        │ │
│  TO THIS INSTITUTION'S RULES                                     │
│  AND REGULATIONS PERTAINING       LESS CASH BACK │     │        │ │
│  TO SAVINGS ACCOUNTS              Total Deposit  │     │        │ │
│     NATIONAL BANK                                                 │
│       Atlanta, GA                                                 │
└─────────────────────────────────────────────────────────────────┘
```

Savings accounts are among the safest vehicles to put money aside for a rainy day, or even a special purpose. But interest earned on these accounts is correspondingly low. That's the price you pay for such low risk.

You can open a savings account with some banks with as little as $100. Some of the larger banks may require a $250 minimum, $500 minimum or more.

When choosing a bank to put your money in make sure that it's FDIC-insured. This means your money is protected up to $100,000, even if the bank is robbed or goes bankrupt. (Yes, even banks file for bankruptcy.)

If a bank you're considering opening an account with *is* FDIC-insured, you'll know because the agency that governs the program (Federal Deposit Insurance Corporation) will have its logo prominently displayed on the front of the building and on all of the bank's literature.

You'll also want to know whether any penalties or fees will be incurred should your account become inactive or fall below a predetermined amount. If you look hard enough, this information is likely to be found wherever there's small print on brochures, flyers and applications — usually at the bottom of the bank's literature.

Check with the following companies to find the best rates nationwide for savings accounts, CDs and other banking products:

100 Highest Yields
P.O. Box 088888
N. Palm Beach, FL 33408-8888

www.Bankrate.com
(800) 327-7717 ext. 11410

Bank Rate Monitor
11760 US Highway 1
Suite 500
N. Palm Beach, FL 33408
www.Bankrate.com
(561) 630-2400

And if you want to get the scoop on the financial wellbeing of a particular bank, get in touch with either or both of the following bank-rating companies:

Veribanc, Inc.
P.O. Box 1610
Woonsocket, RI 02895
www.veribanc.com
(800) 442-2657

Bauer Financial, Inc.
Gable International Plaza
2655 LeJeune Road,
Penthouse One
Coral Gables, FL 33134
www.Bauerfinancial.com
(800) 388-6686

CERTIFICATES OF DEPOSIT

Certificates of deposit (or CDs, as they are better known) are for individuals willing to take on a little more risk. Like savings accounts, CDs are one of the safer banking vehicles. But unlike savings accounts, you give up liquidity (the ability to quickly turn your account into cash) when you put your money in CDs. Your money is tied up in the bank until the maturity date of the CD, which can be anywhere from one month to five years (the legally authorized maximum length of maturity). In return for this inability to access your money, CDs offer more competitive interest rates than do savings accounts or money market accounts (MMAs). More on MMAs later.

If you think you'll need access to your money prior to the stated maturity date, you have two choices: either try to negotiate different terms and conditions, or park your money in a savings or money market account. While you won't earn as much as you would in a CD, at least you won't be penalized for withdrawing your own money.

MONEY MARKET ACCOUNTS/FUNDS

These low-risk, short-term savings options offer competitive rates of interest. Both money market accounts (MMAs) and money market funds (MMFs) invest in similar types of stuff: short-term CDs, commercial paper (short-term, usually low-risk debt issued by large corporations with good credit ratings), bankers' acceptances (short-term credit instruments most commonly used by persons or firms engaged in international trade), treasury bills and notes (short-term debt obligations of the federal government) and Euro dollar loans.

Only MMAs are FDIC-insured because they are bank products. Though there's never been a recorded case of anyone losing money in MMFs, they are not FDIC-insured. They are offerings that were introduced by the mutual fund industry. Most MMAs and MMFs offer limited check-writing features. And with rates comparable to CDs, MMAs and MMFs make good savings vehicles.

STOCKS AND BONDS

It never ceases to amaze me that in the most capitalist nation in the world very few people know even the basics of what stocks and bonds are, what they're used for or how they work. Sure, there are tons of books, magazines, newsletters, websites and television and radio news programs dedicated to these topics. But programs that tout the benefits of investing in the stock market are basically preaching to the converted. In the end, most people are no closer to understanding the securities market than they are to knowing how to manage their money by creating and sticking to a basic household budget.

Stocks and bonds are securities issued by public corporations that need to raise money for working capital in order to expand, pay off debts, etc.

But what exactly are stocks and bonds, and what is a *public* corporation?

Stocks

Simply put, stocks represent equity, or ownership, in a public corporation. When investing in a stock you are essentially investing in the company that issued the stock. This makes you a part owner in the company. If the company makes money, so do you. And if the company loses money, guess what? So do you.

Stocks come in two basic categories: common shares and preferred shares. Common stock shareholders ordinarily have the exclusive right to elect the company's directors, the persons responsible for managing the corporation.

The claims of common shareholders take a back seat or are subordinate to the claims of creditors and other classes of shareholders when liabilities (debt) and dividends (cash or stock a company distributes to shareholders, based on its earnings) are paid, and when assets are distributed upon liquidation or bankruptcy. In return for this subordination, common shareholders have an exclusive claim to the corporation's earnings and assets once other obligations are satisfied.

Preferred shareholders, as the name suggests, have *preference* over common shareholders when it comes to distribution of assets and dividends. Preferred shareholders are customarily given liquidation and dividend preferences over common shareholders. This means that if a company goes bankrupt preferred shareholders will be compensated *before* common shareholders — but after bondholders.

A corporation may have several classes of preferred shares, with one class having preference over another.

Do your homework before investing in a company. Start by following the company in print and broadcast media. Ask yourself what it is about the company you like. The product or services? The way they treat their customers and employees? Their community relations (social responsibility) programs? Their respect for the environment? Indeed, these ought to be some of your basic considerations when planning to invest in a company.

Next, write the company's investor relations department, asking that they send you a copy of their annual (10-K) or quarterly (10-Q) reports. You don't have to be a shareholder of record to get either of these reports. The address for thousands of public (and private) corporations can be found in any of the corporate profile books that "Hoovers" publishes. Ask your facility librarian for reference books that contain the addresses of public corporations.

Of course there's always the Internet. Ask a loved one to assist you in your research efforts. This will make for a learning experience for both of you.

Whatever you do, don't follow hot tips! At the end of the day, the decision on what company to invest in will be yours to make — and it should be an informed one.

Bonds

Bonds are long-term debt instruments (IOUs) that are issued by corporations, municipalities (such as New York City or Los Angeles), and the federal government (and authorized agencies). The issuing company or governmental body is basically borrowing from the bondholder, promising to pay the bondholder a specified amount of interest for a specified length of time, and to repay the loan on the expiration date.

Like stocks, there are different kinds of bonds. Two types are convertible bonds and callable bonds. A convertible bond is one that can, at the option of the holder, be converted into stocks at a predetermined conversion ratio. Callable bonds are bonds that give the issuer the right to pay a specific amount, the call price, to retire the debt obligation before maturity.

MUTUAL FUNDS

Rather than invest directly in a single company, you might prefer mutual funds. These are investment companies that pool money from individuals, pension funds, banks and other institutions to invest in the securities market. Mutual funds invest in everything from stocks and bonds to gold and real estate. As a result, you get built-in diversification.

When you fork over money to a mutual fund you are in essence investing in the fund, not the individual stocks or bonds that the company has chosen to invest in.

Most funds are part of a family of funds, each with its own objectives. For instance, some funds have as their objective a growth or aggressive growth approach. A fund manager heading such a fund would therefore set out to find companies whose stock fits this criterion. Other categories of funds are bond funds, balance funds that consist of both stocks and bonds, and index funds that invest in stocks (or bonds) that make up indices such as the Dow Jones Industrial Average, S&P 500, Russell 2000, or the Wilshire 5000. (These indices track and measure price and trading volume trends of the stocks (or bonds) followed in their respective grouping of stocks or bonds.) There are also value funds that invest in companies whose stocks are considered cheap or undervalued; sector funds that invest in a specific industry or geographical area, such as banks or Japan, respectively; and small- and large-cap funds. Managers of these funds invest based on the size (capitalization) of companies.

With so many funds to choose from (roughly 8,000 in the United States, as of this writing) it can be a daunting task just trying to find a fund that fits your goals and temperament. In addition to looking at past performance (which is no indicator of future performance) you should do your homework on the fund's managers, investment philosophies and its expense ratio (the percentage of income that goes toward covering management and other expenses). An expense ratio of 1% or less is considered reasonable. Index funds have the lowest expense ratios in the mutual fund industry, since very little trading occurs.

Getting Started

Like most novices, you probably think that you have to be rich — or at least have lots of money — to invest in the stock market. Or you may have concluded that investing is simply not for you.

Wrong!

Take a look at the financial section of any newspaper. You'll be surprised to learn how relatively inexpensive it can be to purchase shares of stocks, or to buy corporate bonds. For example, one share of Microsoft would have cost you only $29.86 on December 29, 2006. McDonald's stock closed at $44.33 on the same day. And for $31.58 a share you could've owned a piece of Timberland. For less than a pair of designer jeans, you can own a piece of the above-mentioned (or other well-known) companies.

Get started now. Read everything you can on this stuff. Study stock tables. Establish a practice investment portfolio as you follow stocks over several months.

Seeking Financial Advice

If you think you'll need a lot of handholding, there are full-service brokerage firms that can provide you with everything from research and stock picks to consultation and in-house mutual funds. The two biggest names in the industry are Merrill Lynch and Prudential Securities. Discount brokerages, on the other hand, don't offer as many services as full-service firms. If you've done your own research, already know which stocks you want to buy and don't require handholding, going with a discount broker like E*Trade Financial or Charles Schwab is probably your best bet. For $6.95 you can buy any number of shares from Firstrade Securities.

Online trades can be just as cheap, if not cheaper. E*Trade Financial charges $6.99 - $12.99, depending on the number of trades. TD Ameritrade charges a flat rate of $9.99. And Share Builder charges $1 to $15.95, depending on the number of trades you make.

Cut Out The Middleman

Yet another option that you have at your disposal is to invest in stock (companies) *without* a broker altogether. This means *no* commissions. Yes, it's legal. But because Securities and Exchange Commission rules prohibit these programs from being advertised, the little-known world of Dividend Reinvestment Programs (DRIPs) and Direct Stock Purchase Plans (DSPs) are on the down low.

Over 1,000 publicly held companies (listed on one of the stock exchanges) offer DRIPS or DSPs; many of them are household names like Coca Cola, WalMart, General Electric and McDonalds. Not only is it cheaper (you can start with as little as $50, $100 or $250 — or no minimum — with most programs) than going with a broker, financial planner, or money manager, it's just as easy to get started.

With DRIPS you'll be required to purchase the first share from a broker before joining the company's plan. Not so with DSPs. In this case you can skip the broker altogether. Both programs allow you to automatically reinvest dividends (if the company issues them) in more company shares.

You can find out a great deal more about DRIPS and DSPs — how they work, how to get started, what companies offer them, etc. — by reading either of Charles Carlson's books: "Buying Stocks Without a Broker," or "No-Load Stocks." Information about these programs can also be obtained from Standard & Poor's *Directory of DRIPs*, The National Association of Investors Corporation (NAIC), and the American Association of Individual Investors (AAII).

Whichever route you take, just make sure you do your homework.

chapter 4

LEVERAGE YOUR VISION

HOW MANY TIMES HAVE you told a family member or friend about your plans for the future, only to be met with a blank look, perfunctory smile or nonchalant "yeah, ok"? Probably a bunch of times.

One possible reason for such indifferent responses is that your loved ones may have heard this wide-eyed optimism before. They believed you in the past, when you told them that you were done with prison. That you had learned your lesson and vowed to get a job, go to school, take care of your children, stop using drugs, yadda yadda yadda, when you got out.

Did you keep your word? Maybe…in the beginning. But a few months or years later you landed back in prison — for a second, third or even fourth time. So can you really blame them for not taking you seriously?

Another explanation for their lack of enthusiasm could be that they simply do not share your vision. For one reason or another, they're unable or unwilling to see your future as you see it, or as you want them to see it. Maybe they've got too much on their plates to see beyond their day-to-day responsibilities. Perhaps they just don't believe that you can accomplish the lofty goals you've presented to them. Or, quiet as it's kept, maybe they don't want you to realize your goals, for fear that the relationship they now have with you will change. Whatever, when it comes to convincing others to believe in you and your goals, you've got your work cut out. It's incumbent on you to educate your loved ones, so that they become convinced that you can and will achieve your goals.

MENTORING BEGINS WITH YOU

Many of us were the breadwinners of our households. Even if we made money illegally, our loved ones depended on us to meet their basic needs. They also looked to us for guidance. When we got arrested we left a void in both areas.

Just because you're in prison doesn't mean that your loved ones have stopped looking to you for guidance and support. They haven't. Granted, you're not in a position to provide for your loved ones in a meaningful way financially. But you can still give advice on how they can possibly improve their station in life. And that advice can lead them to embrace your vision. You'd be selfish and irresponsible if you didn't.

But when it comes to discussing your plans to start a business, be mindful that your loved ones initially may not be able to relate to you. This is because in this country we've been programmed to go to school, get a good job and then retire happily ever after. And even though this model is no longer sound, even though unemployment levels are high and the likelihood that many people will not remain at one company (or even two or three) until retirement is even higher, our loved ones can't see beyond the daily grind of work. As worker bees, they live paycheck to paycheck, barely able to make ends meet. Their job has come to mean Just Over Broke.

This is no way to live. Not in America, nor anywhere else. But again, we've been taught to get an education so we can work for others — not ourselves. We've learned to be consumers rather than producers.

Before you can hope to get your loved ones on board with your business aspirations, you'll first have to become a mentor to them. You'll have to hold their hands as you point the way out of a life of joyless, work-induced drudgery.

Begin by initiating conversations (or writing letters) about their job, or their difficulties in finding one. I say this because nine times out of ten, they'll have a lot of pent-up frustration involving their job. It could be that they're not passionate about their work or they dislike a particular co-worker or supervisor. Or, they may not be happy with their pay, lack of health insurance, or any number of other things.

Without sounding manipulative, this is a good time for you to broach the issue of the need for change. Explore with your loved ones some of the benefits of owning their own business: financial freedom, control over how their time is spent and doing what they are passionate about. The idea is to get them to think outside their routine, hapless lives. Take them out of their comfort zone.

To be sure, there will be resistance. Even though they're not happy with their job, and even if they don't have a job, they'll give you one hundred and one reasons why they don't want to start a business: "Wait until you come home." "I'm not cut out for business." "It's too much work." "I hate math, and running a business will mean that I'll have to deal with math." The rationalizations can go on and on.

Don't become discouraged by your loved ones' apprehension. It's normal. In fact, it's actually a healthy response. It suggests that they appreciate the level of commitment, drive and attention to details that owning a business demands.

Use every opportunity to talk about how together you can take charge of your lives. Introduce the subject of starting a business during visits with loved ones, mention it in telephone conversations and include it in your letters to them. After a while they'll realize how serious you are. Or they'll think that you've lost your mind. Whatever…persist. Your enthusiasm may become *their* enthusiasm.

Encourage loved ones to watch financial and business programs on TV, and to visit free web sites. Urge them to read magazine articles and books that focus on entrepreneurship and personal finance. Better yet, send them newspaper and magazine clippings that profile individuals who embarked on one business venture or another. Whenever you hear or read about a business expo that might interest a relative or friend, bring it to their attention. The idea is to get them really interested in and focused on the world of business.

Taking Baby Steps

Don't assume that others will see your vision as clearly as you do. Chances are they won't. After all, it's *your* vision, not theirs. Even if a loved one believes in you and your business idea, they'll still need you to walk them through it — over and over and over again. Be patient, and pace yourself.

Once they've bought into your idea, begin spoon-feeding them the specifics of your business plans. If you run it down all at once, you're likely to overwhelm or even discourage them. Instead, take the time to break your ideas and vision down into manageable, practical step-by-step parts.

For example, let's say you and your loved one decide to start a personalized T-shirt business. Before jumping in with both feet, prepare a checklist of things to do. And be sure to include a timetable.

Here's what your checklist might look like:

BUSINESS INFRASTRUCTURE CHECKLIST

Step 1   Register the business
                            Week of Jan. 1

Step 2   Open a business bank account
                            Week of Jan. 15

Step 3   Have a company logo designed
                            Week of Feb. 2

Step 4   Have logo trademarked
                            Week of Feb. 16

Step 5	Purchase or lease silk-screening equip. Week of March 3
Step 6	Purchase T-shirts Week of March 17
Step 7	Purchase business cards & stationery Week of April 4
Step 8	Secure post office box Week of April 18
Step 9	Have web site designed Week of May 5
Step 10	Obtain sales tax (vendor's) license Week of May 19

Notice that the timetable is spread out over the course of five months. If you were home it might take less than half that time to follow through on the ten steps outlined above. But since you'll be relying on others (who may not be as motivated or diligent as you) to carry out the majority of the legwork, you can expect things to take much longer than you'd like. Indeed, count on things taking two or three times as long as it would if you were home taking care of business yourself. As long as you make consistent progress, that's all that matters.

MICRO STEPS

There may come a time when it seems like you're making little or no progress in getting your business off the ground. It's quite possible that while you were devising your business's infrastructural plan you overlooked some of the small details, what I call *micro steps*. Instead, you focused on the major stuff. There's nothing wrong with this approach. But I strongly suggest that once you've written a general blueprint for jumpstarting your business you should then plug in the micro steps that will take you from one step to the next. The small, neglected details can cause a ripple effect down the line.

The reality is that most incarcerated people operate from a different sense of time than people on the outside. The monotony of prison life is such that when we set out to accomplish something we usually get started right away. We don't ponder or procrastinate. But it's not a matter of filling time or passing time. Often we're trying to make up for lost time, and consequently we experience a sense of urgency. We want to get stuff done quick, fast and in a hurry.

To be sure, your loved ones don't share your sense of urgency. Even though they may support you and your goals, they won't jump when you say jump, move when you say move. This can become very frustrating, to the point where you may feel like abandoning your business plans. Don't! Read your end-goal statement, look for the learning opportunities in the situation and, if possible, get support from organizations like the Small Business Administration, Service Corps of Retired Executives or Small Business Development Centers.

When you feel like giving up, find yourself becoming frustrated or arguing with your loved one about how slow things are going (or their lack of interest), step back for a moment; calm yourself down. Analyze the situation. Try to understand what's actually causing you to feel the way you do. Is it procrastination on the part of a loved one? An unrealistic sense of urgency on your part? Miscommunication? Whatever, work on being more patient — with your loved one, your business's progress and yourself — and on becoming a better listener.

Also, keep in mind that your loved ones have a lot more on their plate than you do. You don't have to get up early every day to drop the kids off at school, go to work, pick the kids up from school, attend PTA meetings and sporting events, go food shopping, do laundry or tend to the kids' emotional and financial needs. Be ever mindful of this whenever you find yourself becoming frustrated.

Have you even thought about whether a loved one you're thinking about going into business with is, in fact, the right person for the job? Just because you love and trust them doesn't mean they're cut out for the long hours and hard work that starting and operating a business demands.

What competencies do they bring to the table? Are they organized? Can they multitask? Do they follow through on tasks? What about computer and research skills? Do they possess them?

You need to conduct this type of skill inventory *before* settling on a particular person to go into business with.

Think for a minute about the times that you've asked a friend or loved one to make a telephone call, relay a message to someone or do something else that you considered to be a simple task, only to be disappointed when they didn't do what they said they would.

This is not to put anyone down. In fact, if there's to be any blame it probably lies in your taking things for granted. Without giving it much thought, you may have assumed that a particular loved one could or would carry out a task when in fact they couldn't. Or wouldn't.

If they *are* willing to help you start a business but are not competent in a certain area, they may be proficient at something else. Here's where asset mapping comes in.

ASSET MAPPING

In a nutshell, asset mapping is a tool that can help determine what skills and aptitudes you and your loved ones currently possess. Think of asset mapping as a skills inventory, a quick way to assess individual and collective strengths and weaknesses.

Knowing in advance what you're good at and what a loved one is good at will make it much easier for you to delegate specific business-related responsibilities. And it'll help you avoid a lot of stress and unnecessary frustration.

You wouldn't want to ask a loved one who's shy and introverted to attend a business expo, just as you'd think twice about designating someone who is computer illiterate to navigate the World Wide Web.

Asset mapping will help you select the right person or persons for the right job.

On a blank piece of paper, draw two or three lines from top to bottom. Write your name at the top of the first column, and the names of each of your loved ones who you hope to go into business with in separate columns. (One name to a column.) Under each name list the skills, aptitudes and other competencies that each person has.

You may discover a few surprises during this exercise. For instance, you may learn that your knack for research complements a loved one's ability to promote and sell the products or services that you intend to offer. You may find out that you have more competencies than you previously thought. Or that a loved one lacks proficiency in several roles that will be needed in the business. In this case you should begin looking outside your familiar network of loved ones and friends.

Indeed, when trying to get others to see and embrace your vision, don't stop at your loved ones. As best-selling author Robert Kiyosaki says, "Business is a team sport."

Don't be too proud to ask for help. Otherwise, you may end up depriving yourself of the wealth of knowledge, assistance and resources that are available to anyone willing to spend a little time exploring them. (You'll find a list of helpful resources in Appendix A.)

Start by writing two or three letters a week to targeted individuals and organizations, asking for specific business information or assistance. Always include a line asking that they refer you to someone who may provide assistance if they themselves cannot. Not every company, agency or person will respond to your letters. But most will.

ITEM 1 (INMATES TEACHING ENTREPRENEURSHIP AND MENTORING)

The implementation of ITEM 1 serves as an example of leveraging *my* vision of bringing entrepreneurial training to incarcerated men and women in New York State.

I'd been reading how-to business books and biographies since 1994, teaching business and personal finance classes since 1995, and by 1999 had been either an active member of or sat on the executive board of several "inmate" organizations. In January 2000, I was elected president of A.C.T. (Association for Community Teamwork), one of several progressive "inmate" organizations at Green Haven Correctional Facility, located in Stormville, New York.

During a discussion at our February 2000 monthly executive board meeting, several of us concluded that most people commit crimes out of a real or imagined need for money, and that when paroled, incarcerated people are likely to end up on one of four tracks: they'll get a job; they'll start a business of their own; they'll wind up on some form of public assistance, or they will resort back to crime.

For us, crime and public assistance were out of the question! As for working for someone else, we looked reality squarely in the face: the truth is that the majority of people leave prison without marketable skills — let alone a G.E.D. This on top of the fact that a criminal conviction puts us at a big disadvantage in the job market.

Weighing our options, we began exploring some of the opportunities that entrepreneurship offers. We began reading business books and magazines and the financial section of newspapers, and we started paying more attention to the business segment of the television evening news.

And, as the universe in its infinite wisdom would have it, I came across an article about Steve Mariotti and his National Foundation for Teaching Entrepreneurship (NFTE). I was inspired by the fact that although he'd been robbed and beaten up by a group of young men while jogging in Manhattan, he'd ultimately confronted his demons by dissolving his import-export business and taking on a job as a teacher in some of the toughest public high schools in New York City.

Steve Mariotti's courage, curiosity and compassion spoke to me. Even more, the fact that he turned a negative experience into a positive outcome made me that much more determined to do the same.

I was determined to not allow prison to break my spirit, determined to not allow prison to rob me of my human potential. And I was determined to have prison serve me — instead of the other way around.

Through A.C.T.'s staff advisor, Laurie Scott, we contacted Steve, inviting him to attend our organization's annual event. Steve not only accepted our invitation, he brought with him valuable books and information. Accompanying him were a number of business luminaries, including John Whitehead, former Deputy Secretary of State in the Reagan Administration. (Mr. Whitehead was later appointed by New York Governor George E. Pataki to serve as chairman of the Lower Manhattan Development Corporation, which oversaw New York City's effort to rebuild downtown after the attack on the World Trade Center.)

In November 2000, I was transferred to Five Points Correctional Facility, a newly built maximum-security prison 300 miles from home. I made written proposals to prison administrators to start an inmate organization whose mission would be to promote self-development and community empowerment. With each proposal, I was told by the deputy superintendent of programs that my application was denied for "insufficient information." And each time I sought clarification as to what specific information was missing. I was given the run-around. So I decided to put my efforts on hold until I was transferred to another prison.

When I arrived at Sullivan Correctional Facility in August 2002, I wasted no time reaching out to Steve. This time I told him about my long-term vision and fervent desire to introduce his entrepreneurship program to my peers so that they could teach their young loved ones.

Within days of writing Steve, I received a copy of his book, "The Young Entrepreneur's Guide to Starting and Running a Business," and a note that read "Let's do it!" We were ready to roll. Or so I thought.

Steve's schedule was busier than I'd imagined, and we had to work around Sullivan's jam-packed in-house calendar of special events. Over the next twenty months, Steve and I went back and forth trying to decide on a suitable date to convene the entrepreneurship seminar. Finally, we settled on May 22, 2004.

With a mix of street savvy and business wit — and a disarming smile — Steve worked the conference room with boundless energy that day. He told the 36 men assembled how he and I met in Green Haven C. F., showed us a video about the National Foundation for Teaching Entrepreneurship (NFTE) and then went into "The Ten Things Every Student Should Know." (Some of them are: develop and maintain good mental and physical health; always do right; goal setting; budgeting; opportunity recognition; financial statements; marketing/sales; business plan summary, and giving back to your community.)

Demand for a full-scale program was evident by the turnout and the rapt attention of the participants. We couldn't stop at just one seminar; we had to take it to the next level.

But before the NFTE program could be taught to the men in Sullivan, some of us would have to undergo five hours of training to become certified instructors.

Based on their commitment to teaching and helping others, and their passion for business, eight men were asked to assist in developing and running the entrepreneurship course under the aegis of NFTE. (Steve came up with the name "Inmates Teaching Entrepreneurship and Mentoring 1." The 1 indicates that Sullivan is the first model of the ITEM program.) All eight accepted, and for three intense months we conducted our own facilitator training.

Official training for ITEM 1 instructors was held on May 28, 2005. Segments were facilitated by Steve, John Whitehead, Landon Hilliard of Brown Brothers Harriman, and Thomas "Tucker" York of Goldman

Sachs. The training enabled us to offer basic entrepreneurship classes to the rest of the prison population.

On November 1, 2005, my fellow certified teachers and I sponsored our first ITEM 1 course. Sixty-two people signed up for the 14-week course but, due to space limitations, only thirty-five men were able to start it. Twenty-five graduated on February 14 and 16, respectively.

On June 24, 2006, we held our first ITEM awards banquet in Sullivan's gymnasium. Seventy-eight people showed up, including Steve Mariotti, John Whitehead and other invited guests.

To us, ITEM 1 represents more than teaching our peers and mentoring youth. We see it as an important tool in reducing recidivism, an important piece in furthering public safety. By giving incarcerated men and women a viable alternative to crime, we enable them to own their personal power and realize their human potential.

Our goal is to first implement ITEM programs throughout New York State's Department of Corrections. We'll then aim to expand our community re-entry model to other states, eventually expanding it nationally. Through entrepreneurship we intend to lift up not only ourselves but our children, families and communities.

PART 2
GETTING DOWN TO BUSINESS

chapter 5

LAWS OF THE LAND

IF NOTHING ELSE, YOU'VE learned that being on the wrong side of the law can have dire consequences — like doing time, with the unrelenting barrage of rules, procedures and regulations that come with it. But just because you plan to get out and go legit doesn't mean there won't be rules to follow. There will be. So you had better do your homework to find out what statutes, local rules or government agency regulations might apply to you and your specific business situation.

The good news is that we live in a free-enterprise system. This means businesses are privately owned (as opposed to state-run) and almost anyone can operate a business relatively free of government interference.

Other than curfews and the nature of your crime, there are no parole-specific barriers to starting a business. Sure, your parole officer may not think it's a good idea for you to start a business. He or she may even become envious and resent your ambitions. If you encounter animosity or resistance from your parole officer, try to get reassigned to a different, more cooperative parole officer. If that doesn't work, don't get discouraged. Think of this as temporary and keep your eyes on the prize.

And whatever you do in your zeal to start your business, don't quit your job (assuming you have one). Start a part-time, home-based business at first. As long as you're working, reporting to your parole officer and attending any mandated offense-related programs (i.e. drugs, violence, parenting), you'll be operating within the boundaries of the law.

Licenses: Mandatory and Discretionary Bars

Before embarking on any business, do your homework. Find out what licenses, permits or certificates you'll need to start or operate your business. Having a felony conviction (and, in some cases, a misdemeanor) may prevent you from obtaining certain licenses and permits.

There are three categories of state licensing laws: those that preclude licensure on the basis of a criminal conviction (these are mandatory bars), those that restrict licenses by requiring an applicant to have good moral character, or trustworthiness (discretionary bars) and, finally, those that do not restrict licensing based on prior bad acts. Appendix D contains a list of occupations in New York State which require some type of license or permit.

Licensure of Persons Who've Been Convicted of One or More Criminal Offenses

Generally speaking, it is the public policy of many states to encourage the licensure of formerly incarcerated persons. A conviction of a crime won't automatically bar you from obtaining a professional license. Each application for professional licensure is supposed to be reviewed on its own merits.

The nature of your criminal conviction and its relationship to the profession in which you seek licensure will be evaluated at the time you've satisfied all other requirements for licensure. By law the licensing agency cannot (at least in theory) unfairly discriminate or deny your application based on the fact that the nature of one or more of your previous convictions has some relationship to the license being sought. Your convictions must bear a *direct* relationship to the specific license that you apply for. So if your conviction was for robbery, you can forget about getting a certificate of registration as a mortgage broker. If your conviction was for drugs or a sexual offense, expect to be denied any license that allows you to work around or with children. (This doesn't apply to mandatory forfeitures of disabilities imposed by law.) The licensing agency can, however, deny your application by determining that issuing you a license "would involve an unreasonable risk to property or to the safety or welfare of specific individuals or the general public."

Another sticking point that could be used (usually in conjunction with other considerations) to reject your licensing application is a finding that you lack "good moral character." This is one of those generic phrases that is determined and applied subjectively. Evidently, the "good moral character" clause is a loophole that allows licensing agencies to deny your application. The determination is made on a case-by-case basis.

Case in point: On March 4, 2005, *The New York Times* ran an article about the dilemma of Marc La Cloche, a formerly incarcerated person who, while in prison, spent most of his time learning the trade of barbering. Upon release, he applied for a state license to become a barber. He was initially denied a license. But the decision was later reversed, and he worked as a barber in a barbershop. If only that was how the story ended.

New York State's Secretary of State successfully appealed the decision, Mr. La Cloche's barbering license was revoked, and that was the end of his labor of love. All because an administrative judge ruled that the applicant's criminal history "indicate (d) a lack of good moral character and trustworthiness for licensing."

Mr. La Cloche died of AIDS-related complications in 2006, months after the revocation of his barbering license.

In New York State, there are eight factors that must be considered regarding a previous criminal conviction (some variation of these is likely to apply to other states):

1. *Public policy.* Like some other states, New York's public policies encourage licensure of people with felony convictions. Others do not. Twenty-five states and the District of Columbia have no standards governing the relevance of felony convictions

of applicants seeking occupational licenses. This may sound good, but it actually means that the licensing agencies in these states don't need a reason to deny your applications. These states are: Alabama, Alaska, Georgia, Idaho, Illinois, Iowa, Maine, Maryland, Massachusetts, Mississippi, Nevada, New Hampshire, North Carolina, Ohio, Oklahoma, Rhode Island, South Carolina, South Dakota, Tennessee, Texas, Utah, Vermont, Virginia, West Virginia and Wyoming.

The other 25 states *do* have standards that require a "direct," "rational" or "reasonable" relationship between the license sought and the applicant's criminal history to justify denial of a license.

2. *The specific duties and responsibilities necessarily related to the license sought.* You can be denied a particular license based on the type of duties or responsibilities that you'd have to carry out. For instance, installing or repairing alarm systems is out of the question.

3. *The bearing, if any, the criminal offense or offenses for which the person was previously convicted will have on his fitness or ability to perform one or more such duties or responsibilities.* Say your felony conviction stemmed from an assault on a child. You're likely to be denied a license as an operator of a child daycare center.

4. *The time which has elapsed since the occurrence of the criminal offense or offenses.* The longer the amount of time that has passed since the commission of the crime, the less likely you are to repeat the same offense. At least in theory. If, say, your crime was committed ten years ago, all else being equal, you'd have a better shot at securing a license than someone whose crime occurred a year ago.

5. *The age of the person at the time of occurrence of the criminal offense or offenses.* As with the length of time that has gone by since the criminal offense or offenses occurred, if you were very young when you committed the offense and are now much older, this will be to your advantage when applying for a license.

6. *The seriousness of the offense or offenses.* There's nothing you can do to change the nature or seriousness of your conviction(s). If your offense or offenses were violent, the licensing agency will most likely give this fact considerable weight in making its determination to grant or deny your application.

7. *Any information produced by the person, or produced on his behalf, in regard to his rehabilitation and good conduct.* The sooner you begin gathering letters of support and other character endorsements, the better. In fact, this should be an ongoing process.

8. *The legitimate interest of the public agency in protecting property, and the safety and welfare of specific individuals or the general public.* This is another one of those general, subjective criterion in the decision-making process. If your conviction was for a violent or property-related crime, this fact will negatively affect your chances of getting a license. If you've received a certificate of relief from disabilities or a certificate of good conduct, the public agency must also consider this fact. (More about this below.)

Discretionary Relief From Forfeitures and Civil Disabilities

Luckily, some states provide formerly incarcerated individuals with a *limited* form of relief from forfeitures and civil disabilities, including licensing; New York is one such state. Consult your state's licensing authorities to determine what their public policy is as it relates to licensure of formerly incarcerated persons.

In New York State, if you have only one felony or misdemeanor conviction, you can apply for a "Certificate of Relief from Disability." This certificate is designed to remove specific civil disabilities — or incapacities for the full enjoyment of ordinary legal rights — automatically imposed when you were convicted. (Examples are denial of such privileges as voting, holding public office and obtaining many jobs and occupational licenses.) In essence, it reinstates those privileges.

Issuance of a Certificate of Relief from Disability is at the discretion of the sentencing court or the New York State Board of Parole, based on the favorable character or fitness of the individual applicant. It is granted as long as the relief is consistent with the rehabilitation of the eligible person and with public interest.

If you were sentenced to more than one year in a New York State Correctional Facility, a Certificate of Relief from Disability must be obtained directly from the New York State Parole Board. On the other hand, if you were sentenced to not more than one year in a county jail (or if you were granted conditional discharge or probation) you must apply for a Certificate of Relief from Disability from the court that sentenced you.

Certificates of Good Conduct are for individuals who have two or more felony convictions (or any number of misdemeanors). On top of having to demonstrate that you are rehabilitated, there's a mandatory waiting period, based on your most serious conviction, that prescribes when you can apply for a Certificate of Good Conduct. If your most serious conviction was for a class "C," "D," or "E" felony, you'll have to wait at least three years from the date of your last conviction, payment of fine or release from prison to parole supervision (or post-release supervision) before applying for a Certificate of Good Conduct. If your most serious conviction was for a class "A" or "B" felony you will have to wait at least five years.

When you apply for a Certificate of Good Conduct, your application must be notarized and returned with proof of payment of income taxes and W2 tax forms (if you've worked during the previous three years). The State Parole Board will review your application and assign it to a local parole officer, who will conduct an investigation, including a visit to your home. The parole officer will then forward his or her recommendation to the State Parole Board, which will make the final decision and notify you by mail. The process from beginning to end can take from six months to a year.

Remember, issuance of either type of certificate is discretionary; and even when it is issued, it won't prevent an administrative or licensing authority from exercising its discretionary powers to suspend, revoke or refuse to renew any license.

Other Civil Liabilities

Concerned with incarcerated persons profiting from their crimes, some state legislatures have enacted civil liabilities related to criminal offenses. In 1977, New York became the first state to enact a "Son of Sam" law. It was passed in response to public outrage amid widespread speculation that publishers would offer huge sums of money to David Berkowitz, the so-called "Son of Sam" who was convicted of six murders, for his story. Other states followed suit.

Initially, only the proceeds from the sale of books, magazines, motion pictures or other media exploitations of crimes were denied incarcerated persons. Proceeds had to be paid instead to the Crime Victims Board (CVB) for the benefit of the victims of the crime or their surviving family members. The New York State laws were greatly extended in 2001, with amendments that now allow crime victims to sue you (in some cases even while you are out on parole) for *any* money and property that you receive from *any* source.

Ordinarily, under the state's civil practice and rules, crime victims (or the CVB) would be required to file a suit against you within a seven-year statute of limitations. However, the 2001 amendment expanded the statute of limitations to run for up to three years from the time the crime victim learns of your coming into possession of payments or property valued at $10,000 or more — from any source. The law cannot be circumvented by your receiving the money in a series of installments that, combined, total more than $10,000. The only sources of money that are exempt are child support owed and earned income.

That's not all: anyone who receives on your behalf money (or property) that exceeds $10,000 must notify the CVB. Otherwise, they risk being severely fined or having other penalties imposed.

Once the crime victim notifies the CVB that he wants to initiate a suit against you, the board will promptly seek injunctive relief from the courts to prevent you from spending any of your money.

Under New York State's "Son of Sam Law," the following can be assessed as compensation for victims of crimes in all civil judgments obtained against you:

1. Any amount above the first $1,000 deposited in your DOCS account,
2. Up to 90% of compensatory damages you might be awarded if you win a case you bring to court, or
3. 100% (that's right, all!!!) of punitive damages you might be awarded in such a case.

WHAT ABOUT GOVERNMENT GRANTS FOR FORMERLY INCARCERATED PERSONS WANTING TO START A BUSINESS?

You may have heard that after serving five or more years in prison you will be considered socially and economically disbled and, as a result, you'll be entitled to monies (in the form of grants or loans) from the government to start a business.

Point blank, this is just a rumor. Despite the wide-ranging scope of the rumor, it simply is not true. Sorry to burst your bubble, but there are *no* government grants directly available to formerly incarcerated persons to start a business. Nor are there any government loan programs in existence for this purpose.

PRISON ENTREPRENEURSHIP PROGRAM

Over the last few years, a number of nonprofit organizations have been formed to teach incarcerated persons (and formerly incarcerated persons) the ins and outs of starting and operating their own businesses. The Prison Entrepreneurship Program (PEP), based in Byron, Texas, is one such organization. Founded in 2004 by Catherine Rohr, who was inspired by Charles W. Colson's prison ministry, the nonprofit plans to expand to other prisons in the Texas system, as well as to the California and New York State systems.

Make no mistake about it, Mrs. Rohr's PEP is not for the faint of heart. Before being accepted into her four-month program, applicants are interviewed eleven times, nine of them by their peers. Program participants take up to five tests during the course, read Steve Mariotti's book "How to Start and Operate a Small Business" in three weeks, and write comprehensive business plans.

There's also an Executive Mentoring component that gives formerly incarcerated graduates of PEP access to financing. The program has been a success, with only four out of 165 graduates returning to prison.

chapter 6

WHY BUSINESSES FAIL

T HE PLAIN TRUTH IS that many businesses fail within their first few years of existence. According to a May 2005 study, "Survival and Longevity in the Business Employment Dynamics Database," by Amy E. Knaup (Monthly Labor Review, Volume 128, Number 5), one-third (or 33%) of new employer establishments fail within two years. The failure rate jumps significantly, to 56%, during the next two years. Said differently, almost six out of ten new businesses fail within the first four years. Obviously business isn't for everyone. There are myriad reasons why so many businesses fail.

FAILURE AS TEACHER

Knowing beforehand why some businesses fail can put you ahead of the pack. You'll have the advantage of learning from other people's mistakes, sparing yourself wasted time and energy, and bouts of frustration and discouragement.

Here are some reasons — and lessons — for why many businesses fail:

- *Not enough money*. More businesses fail because they lack sufficient finances than any other reason. I'm not only talking about inadequate finances to start a business, but about enough working capital to sustain the business during the first several months (and possibly years) of operation.
  Lesson: Don't fool yourself into thinking that your great

business idea alone will be enough to catapult your business to the million-dollar level. Carefully plan realistic start-up costs and projected income statements.

- *Poor cash flow.* It's easy to assume that since sales are being made — even a lot of sales — that your business is profitable and is meeting financial obligations. No matter how much a business brings in in sales, if it cannot keep up with satisfying debt and other financial obligations as they arise it will have poor cash flow. This situation could expose your company to the possibility of bankruptcy or arbitration by creditors.
  Lesson: Keep track of cash inflows and outflows of your business. It all boils down to being able to pay your debts and satisfy other obligations — and, hopefully, make a profit.

- *Half-assed planning.* Many businesses fail within the first few years of operation because their owners take the road of least resistance: they fail to thoroughly plan their business. Most do not prepare a business plan. It's no wonder they experience a shortage of money (or cash flow problems) to keep the business afloat.
  Lesson: If you fail to plan…well, you know the rest. Taking the time — before going into business — to write a solid business plan will reveal whether your idea is even feasible.

- *Lacking a clearly defined niche.* Too many businesses are Johnny-come-latelys. Their owners are trend followers, not leaders or mavericks. As a result, these businesses don't stand out in the crowd.
  Lesson: If you don't give customers a clear reason to buy from you, they won't.

- *Vague marketing.* Thinking that it will increase sales, some businesses cast too wide a net and try to be all things to all customers. Or they fail to properly position their company and its products and services.

Lesson: Make it easy for customers to see the need and want to buy from *your* business, as opposed to someone else's.

- *Slow moving and/or bureaucratic*. Perhaps due to the owner's personality, or the big size of a business, some companies have a delayed reaction when it comes to responding to market, product/service or legal demands or trends.
  Lesson: Don't be afraid to experiment. If a product or service or any other aspect of your business isn't working out, do something differently. Never let the size of your business slow you down.

- *Lack of follow-up*. Concerned about "the sale," too many businesses ignore the importance of ongoing customer satisfaction and retention.
  Lesson: How you treat your customers when they're *not* making purchases may be more important than what you sell them.

- *Wearing too many hats*. Running a business is no easy undertaking. Out of fear of sharing the reigns, or plain ignorance, some small business owners try to do it all. Often they end up burning out or failing miserably at certain tasks.
  Lesson: Play to your strengths. Don't try to be a Jack (or Jill) of all trades. Hire others (or outsource) to do those tasks that you don't enjoy doing or are simply not good at.

- *Inexperienced or unmotivated employees*. Assuming the business will practically run itself, some misguided businessowners put little effort or resources into hiring qualified employees. Or, once hired, the employees aren't kept motivated.
  Lesson: Hiring and retaining good employees should be taken seriously. Everything about your business, including the

"quality" of your employees, represents your company's brand in the eyes of customers, suppliers and partners. Properly train them, pay them well and make them feel valued.

- *Unmanageable growth.* Swept away by the excitement of booming demand, some businesses grow too fast. When customers knock on their doors (or make purchases online) they have no product or service to offer them. They're overwhelmed, understocked, understaffed or underfunded. *Lesson*: It's a mistake to assume that rapid growth is automatically a good thing. If your company is unable to meet consumer demand or satisfy debt or other obligations in a timely fashion, what initially seemed like a boom can just as easily turn into a bust. Track and manage your business growth trajectory.

chapter 7

YOUR GAME PLAN

S URELY YOU'VE HEARD OF the 5 Ps: Proper preparation prevents poor performance. This adage is certainly applicable when it comes to drafting a comprehensive business plan. No doubt, a lot of businesses are started without an official plan. In fact, I'll hazard a guess that most businesses do not start out with a written plan that describes and analyzes their business, a plan that provides detailed projections about the business's future.

The more successful businesses *do* have business plans, very detailed ones. They don't leave their ultimate success to chance. And neither should you.

WHY WRITE A BUSINESS PLAN

More than anything, a good business plan serves as a feasibility test. It'll help you determine whether your concept is realistic and doable — saving you a lot of time, money and effort trying to get your business off the ground. Without a well-thought- out business plan, the likelihood of your overlooking critical aspects of your business is elevated.

Taking the time to research your ideas and prepare a plan will improve your odds of success. Going through this process allows you to think through your business concept in ways that you can't if you rush to draft a plan (or fail to draft one at all.)

Another benefit of writing a business plan *before* you actually go into business is that once you open up shop your plan will help you track your progress — or lack of progress. A business plan is meant to be dynamic, to be revised and updated as your business experiences growth spurts and lulls.

Finally, if you think you'll need to borrow money (whether from relatives, friends, bankers or venture capitalists) to start or expand your business, a business plan will be indispensable. Don't wait until you actually need financing to write a business plan. From the outset, you should talk about your business goals and objectives with relatives and friends, nurture relationships with potential lenders and devise a solid game plan.

BUSINESS PLAN COMPONENTS

There's no precise number of pages that a business plan ought to have. It all depends on the nature of your business and the complexity of the concept behind it. Likewise, it might take a few days to write your plan, or it could just as well take up to six months.

In most instances, a basic business plan can be broken down into eight sections or components: cover page, table of contents, executive summary, business description, management plan, operations plan, marketing plan and financial plan.

Let's explore each component.

1. *Cover page*: On this page include the name of the business, the names of the person(s) who wrote the business plan (with contact information), and the date that the plan was completed or revised.
2. *Table of contents*: This comes immediately after your cover page. Basically it should list all the sections and subsections of your business plan, along with their respective page numbers so they're easy to locate.
3. *Business description*: This section tells readers of your plan what your business is about. It spells out the type of business it is

(retail, wholesale, service or manufacturer), the business's goals, purpose and/or mission, and who the owners of the business are or will be. Also included in the business description is the legal structure of the business, its location and status (i.e., start-up, ongoing, expansion or buying), and detailed information about the industry that the business is in.

4. *Management plan*: Hands down, this will probably be the section of your business plan that prospective lenders will pay the most attention to. After all, the business will not run itself. Sure, lenders will want to know how much money you're trying to raise and for what purposes. They will no doubt need to know how and when you intend to repay them — with interest, of course! But ultimately it's the people who will actually run your business who'll particularly interest lenders. In this section you'll want to put management personnel (Including an organizational chart with titles of company officers will make you look professional and, well, organized.), as well as the names and contact information of directors or advisors, if applicable.

State the number of full- and part-time employees. Expound on how and where you will find and keep employees, and how much you will pay them. Do you intend to offer employees benefits like flextime, medical insurance or retirement plans? If so, note this fact in your management plan, along with estimates of the cost of these benefits.

What about employee training? Will it be necessary, and if so, who will conduct the actual training? How and where will the training be conducted? And how much will it cost? If any of the above scenarios apply to your business, make sure you include satisfactory explanations in your management plan.

5. *Operations plan*: Where will your business initially be located? Will it be home-based or in a retail district or mall? If there are any zoning laws that apply to your business, note them in your operations plan. Also include the days and hours that your business will operate. List your vendors and suppliers,

and operations/functions that you intend to outsource. Finally, if any special equipment or processes will be used in your business be sure to mention this in this section of your plan.

6. *Marketing plan*: In this section, the first thing you must obviously do is define your target market. Provide a detailed market analysis, spelling out the demographics, geographics and psychographics (the breakdown of prospective customers by their motivations and behavior patterns) of your ideal market. Break down the competition and your competitive advantage. What are your marketing objectives and strategies? How much will it cost to implement your marketing strategy, and what is your projected return on investment? Over what length of time will your marketing goals and objectives be in effect? How will you measure progress? Also talk about the overall industry and trends.

   You can get a lot of market research mileage out of a good library. There you'll find all sorts of books, magazines and trade publications related to the industry your business is in. If you have access to the Internet, all the better. Another possibility is to put together a focus group of individuals who fit the profile of your target market. Finally, you can conduct surveys or questionnaires, which will provide valuable feedback.

7. *Financial plan*: Words are one thing but numbers tell their own story. How much start-up capital will you need and for what purposes? If you'll need to borrow money, exactly how much will you need? How do you intend to pay the money back? How much of your own money will you put up? You should also include projections of the costs of goods (or services) sold, operating costs and financial statements (two or three years of personal income tax returns and a business balance sheet, income statement and cash-flow statement).

chapter 8

CHOOSING THE RIGHT BUSINESS STRUCTURE

T HE FACT THAT YOU'VE read this far suggests that you are serious about starting a business and becoming a successful entrepreneur. You are now ready to do the damn thing.

In Chapter 7, "Your Game Plan," you learned how to outline and write a solid business plan. Now it's time to implement your plan, to get down to the nuts and bolts of it all.

What word comes to mind when you think of business or legal structures? I'll bet the word is *corporation*. The words *business* and *corporation* seem to be synonymous. This is misleading because most businesses are registered as sole proprietorships — not corporations.

Another misconception is that all corporations are huge, publicly held and therefore on the New York Stock Exchange. This just isn't true. In fact, the exact opposite is more the reality. That is, the vast majority of businesses registered as corporations are relatively small. They have fewer than 500 employees and gross under $6.5 million. They are either owned by family members, friends or a small network of associates — not by the public at large.

The reasons most businesses are structured as sole proprietorships are explained below in *Pros and Cons of Business Structures.*

THINGS TO CONSIDER WHEN
CHOOSING A BUSINESS STRUCTURE

What are your short- and long-term personal and business goals? What are your primary concerns? Is it taxation? Estate planning? The effect that an owner's death or withdrawal would have on the business? Whatever it is, you need to think about what's most important to you and your loved ones *before* considering what type of business structure would be best for a particular business.

Then, once you're ready to explore business structures, understand that there's no one-size-fits-all model. You might want to use a process of elimination to decide which model best suits your needs. In other words, go over the list of pros and cons of each business structure. As you do this, eliminate or cancel out those that would not suit you, your loved ones or other business partners.

Determine which will best accommodate what you want to accomplish. (More about this later.)

Some types of businesses are better off, for tax and managerial purposes, as a limited partnership than as a corporation or limited liability company (LLC). For example, real estate investment companies and some oil-producing companies are just two types of businesses that lend themselves to being structured as limited partnerships. The reason for this is that instead of requiring hands-on partners to help run the business, limited partnerships need only investment capital. The general partners manage the day-to-day business.

So just what are some of the things you ought to consider when choosing your business's legal structure? Start by figuring out which structure best serves your needs when it comes to:

1. Protection of family assets and investments
2. Management control
3. Avoiding family disputes
4. Flexibility of decision making
5. Succession of children and other family members to

     management
6. The nature of the business to be operated
7. The nature of the assets to be held
8. The number of owners involved
9. Estate planning and gifting of assets
10. Who may legally obligate the business
11. Effect upon an owner's death or withdrawal
12. The need for start-up funding
13. Taxation
14. Privacy of ownership
15. Consolidation of assets and investments
16. Legal restrictions
17. Intended division of earnings

Six Primary Business Structures

If all this talk about process of elimination and choosing one business structure over another has your head spinning, welcome to the club. As you now know, there's a lot that has to be taken into consideration before deciding which legal structure to choose for your business.

Generally speaking, there are six primary business structures from which to choose. Seven if you count not-for-profit corporations.

Sole Proprietorship

As the name suggests, a sole (or single) proprietorship is owned by one person. The owner may decide to hire employees or run the business by himself or herself.

General Partnership

When two or more business owners go into business together, sharing in the profits, losses and day-to-day responsibilities, they form what's called a general partnership. (A Partnership Agreement should be drafted — preferably by an experienced attorney — to spell out the rights and responsibilities of each partner.)

Limited Partnership (LP)

Unlike general partnerships, partners in a limited partnership don't have a say in how the business will operate. In essence, limited partners are investors in a limited partnership. And since they have no say in the day-to-day operations, their liability for debt is limited. In order for a business to exist as a limited partnership, there must be at least one *general* partner, who is liable for all partnership debts.

Limited Liability Company (LLC)

This relatively new business structure combines the advantages of partnerships and corporations. That is, income is taxed only once, as the personal income of members, and personal assets are protected from lawsuits. And like regular C-Corporations, they don't have the legal restrictions of S-Corporations.

Regular C-Corporation

Under the laws of the United States, a corporation is a legal *person* distinct from that of its owners. As such, a corporation can have its own name, can sue and be sued in its own name, and has the right to buy, sell, lease and mortgage its property in its own name. Corporations are classified as either public or private.

Public corporations have shares that are widely dispersed. Except in the limited situations where there's an exemption from filing with the Securities and Exchange Commission (SEC), a corporation becomes public only after an underwriting process, often called IPO, or Initial Public Offering.

A private or closely-held corporation is one whose shares, or at least voting shares, are held by a single shareholder or closely-knit group of shareholders, usually family members.

S-Corporation

S-Corporations are taxed only once, as the personal income of shareholders. Unlike regular C-Corporations, though, S-Corporations have a number of legal restrictions, as you will see on page 99.

Nonprofit Corporation

These are also called 501 (c) (3) corporations because of the section of the Internal Revenue Code that governs them. The federal government affords nonprofits tax-exemption because the products or services they provide are not intended for profit-making purposes. Instead, they strive to contribute to the welfare of society. Their objectives are charitable or benevolent.

Now that the various business structures have been defined, let's go right into the pros and cons of each.

Sole Proprietorship

Pros
- Easiest and least expensive form of ownership to organize.
- Owner has complete control over business; he or she makes all management decisions.
- Owner receives all profits.
- Profits from business flow directly to owner's personal income tax return. Losses are deductible without limit on personal tax return.
- The business is easy to dissolve.

Cons
- Owner assumes unlimited liability; business *and* personal assets are at risk.
- Sole proprietorships are at a disadvantage when it comes to raising funds (because lenders generally consider it risky to depend on one person's ability to satisfy a loan compared to

expecting repayment from, say, a partnership or corporation's assets).

- Owner may have difficulty attracting high-caliber employees, particularly those wanting an ownership stake in the company.
- Owner is responsible for running all aspects of the business.
- Owner interest is not easily transferable.
- The business is automatically dissolved upon the death of the owner.

General Partnership

Pros

- Easy to establish.
- Benefits from strengths, skills and resources of partners.
- Individual partners are taxed on their share of business income on personal tax returns. Losses are deductible without limit.

Cons

- Each partner is *personally* liable for entire amount of any business debt or claim — even if incurred by other partner or partners.
- Management decisions are divided, which could lead to disagreements.
- Partnership may dissolve upon withdrawal or death of partner.

Limited Partnership (LP)

Pros

- For general partners, losses are deductible without limit on personal income tax.
- Limited Partnership does *not* dissolve upon death or withdrawal of limited partner.

- General partner can own as little as 1% of limited partnership and yet have 100% control over management.
- Creditors can only place claims on the partnership assets and assets of general partner.

Cons

- Limited partners may lose their limited liability status if they manage *any* aspect of the business.
- Limited partner may deduct on personal tax returns share of losses *only* to the extent of their investment.
- Limited partnership may dissolve upon death or withdrawal of general partner.
- General or limited partner's rights or interest may not be wholly transferable.

Limited Liability Company (LLC)

Pros

- Easier to form than a corporation.
- No limit on number or type of business owners.
- Liability of members is limited to members' personal investment.
- Flexible allocation of profits and losses.
- Flexible management structure: member or manager management.

Cons

- Much more complex tax filing system.
- Tax and liability treatment is *not* uniform; it varies from state to state.
- Restrictions may be placed on transfer of ownership.
- May be dissolved upon death or withdrawal of member.

Regular C-Corporation

Pros
- Ownership and management may be completely separate.
- Shareholders' liability is limited to personal investment.
- Corporations may exist in perpetuity. They never have to be dissolved.
- Shareholders may sell without limit unless a contrary agreement exists.
- Corporations can attract lots of money.

Cons
- Requires more time and money to establish than other forms of organization.
- More paperwork required to comply with regulations.
- Subject to corporate taxation.
- May be subject to double taxation, if dividends are issued to shareholders.

S-Corporation

Pros
- Ownership and management may be completely separate.
- Shareholders' liability is limited to personal investment.
- Losses are deductible on personal income tax return.
- No dissolution upon death or withdrawal of owners (shareholders).

Cons
- Maximum of 100 shareholders.
- *All* shareholders must be either U.S. citizens or permanent resident aliens.
- Shares may *only* be owned by individuals, estates and certain types of trusts.
- Must have issued only one class of stock.

- Will lose S-Corporation status if *any* legitimate shareholder sells to any prohibited shareholder.
- No more than 25% of S-Corporation's gross income can be derived from passive investment activities, such as real estate or stocks and bonds.

Nonprofit Corporation

Pros
- Possible tax-exempt status.
- Donations may be tax-deductible.
- May solicit funding and/or sponsorship from federal, state and local government entities, as well as corporate and individual sponsors.
- May invest in other businesses.

Cons
- Usually has to rely on grants and donations.
- Not permitted to issue stock.
- Must adhere to a lot of regulations.
- Salaries for corporation officers are much lower than salaries at comparable for-profit entities.
- There are no shares of stock, so no one has an ownership stake in the corporation.

REGISTERING YOUR BUSINESS

Don't confuse registering your business with actually operating it. Registering your business is merely the preliminaries, the first couple of steps of setting up shop. The heavier lifting comes with day-to-day operations. Below is the step-by-step process of registering each of the seven business structures mentioned earlier.

Sole Proprietorship

Step 1:   Conduct a business name search at the County Clerk's office to make sure the name of your business is not already being used.

Step 2:   Purchase DBA (Doing Business As) forms from a commercial stationery store.

Step 3:   Fill out three forms, then take them to the County Clerk's office where your business will be located.

Step 4:   Have DBA forms notarized and pay court filing fee.

General Partnership

Step 1:   Conduct a business name search at the County Clerk's office to make sure the name of your business is not already being used.

Step 2:   Purchase DBA (Doing Business As) forms from a commercial stationery store.

Step 3:   Fill out three forms, then take them to the County Clerk's office where your business will be located.

Step 4:   Have DBA forms notarized and pay court filing fee.

Limited Partnership

Step 1:   Have your state's Department of State (or whatever agency serves your state's business community) conduct a business name search to make sure the name of your business is not already being used.

Step 2:   Purchase "Certificate of Limited Partnership" forms from a commercial stationery store.

Step 3:   Fill out the forms and send one copy to your state's Department of State.

Step 4:   Within 120 days after filing with the Department of State, publish each week for six successive weeks a notice in two newspapers in the county where the business is located, specifying the details of the limited partnership.

Limited Liability Company

Step 1: Have your state's Department of State conduct a business name search to make sure the name of your business is not already being used.

Step 2: Purchase "Articles of Organization" forms from a commercial stationery store.

Step 3: Fill out the forms and send one copy to your state's Department of State.

Step 4: Within 120 days after filing with the Department of State, publish each week for six successive weeks a notice in two newspapers in the county in which the business is located, specifying the details of the limited liability company.

S-Corporation

Step 1: Have your state's Department of State conduct a business name search to make sure the name of your business is not already being used.

Step 2: Purchase a "Certificate of Incorporation" form from the Department of State or a commercial stationery store.

Step 3: Fill out the "Certificate of Incorporation" and send a copy to the Department of State with the filing fee.

Step 4: File form #2553, "Election by a Small Business Corporation," with the IRS.

Step 5: Once the IRS grants approval for your corporation to exist as an S-Corporation, you must then file a separate form with your state's Department of Taxation and Finance (or whatever name it goes by).

Regular C-Corporation

Step 1: Have your state's Department of State conduct a business name search to make sure the name of your business is not already being used.

Step 2:   Purchase a "Certificate of Incorporation" form from the Department of State or a commercial stationery store.

Step 3:   Fill out the "Certificate of Incorporation" and send a copy to the Department of State with the filing fee.

Nonprofit Corporation

Step 1:   Have your state's Department of State conduct a business name search to make sure the name of your business is not already being used.

Step 2:   Apply for and secure any required consents and/or approvals from state agencies that regulate the type of business you're starting.

Step 3:   Purchase a "Certificate of Incorporation" form from the Department of State or a commercial stationery store.

Step 4:   Fill out the "Certificate of Incorporation" form and send the completed form with any consents/approvals you've obtained from applicable state agencies, and the filing fee, to the Department of State.

Step 5:   Seek federal and state tax-exempt status from the IRS and State Department of Taxation and Finance, respectively.

chapter 9

SOCIAL ENTREPRENEURSHIP

WITH MORE THAN 650,000 men and women leaving state and federal prisons each year, and most needing some type of assistance in their re-entry process, there are numerous and varied opportunities to address their unique needs. Said another way, 650,000 men and women being paroled annually makes for a "market" of formerly incarcerated persons.

Let's say you want to open and operate a job-training facility for formerly incarcerated persons, or a halfway house that provides drug counseling and life skills to its residents. After all, you may not be interested in becoming rich or famous. Instead your mission may be to make a difference in people's lives.

Some of the services you might consider providing this market are:

- Employment
- Job/vocational training
- Entrepreneurship training/support
- G.E.D./college courses
- Life skills (budgeting, banking, technology, etc.)
- Transitional or permanent housing
- Mental health services
- Family counseling
- Marriage counseling

- Drug counseling
- HIV/AIDS counseling
- Mentoring
- Health insurance

Through *social* entrepreneurship it's possible for you to earn a decent living (you probably won't get rich) *and* provide much-needed services to underserved communities.

WHAT IS SOCIAL ENTREPRENEURSHIP?

The term "social entrepreneurship" was coined by Bill Drayton, the founder and CEO of "Ashoka," a nonprofit organization that identifies and invests in leading social entrepreneurs. Social entrepreneurship is the act of identifying and solving social problems such as poverty, crime and teenage drug addiction. Visionaries in this field use both traditional and innovative approaches to bring about social change.

THE INDEPENDENT SECTOR

Organizations that are neither governmental nor business fall under what's sometimes referred to as the independent sector, or the third sector. In the United States the term often used is the not-for-profit sector. Outside the United States these institutions are called nongovernmental organizations, or NGOs.

Whichever name they go by, the general purpose of these organizations is to improve the social fabric of a community, region of a state or country, or an entire country. Nonprofits can take the form of charities, foundations, social welfare organizations or professional and trade associations.

Nonprofit corporations are exempt from taxes primarily because they provide valuable services to society and relieve the government of services it might otherwise have to offer.

WHO OWNS A NONPROFIT?

No one owns a nonprofit corporation in the way that shareholders actually own a for-profit corporation. The nonprofit corporation has no shareholders. Its officers and other employees may receive reasonable compensation for services rendered but, unlike a for-profit entity, corporate assets or profits cannot be distributed to them.

While no one actually owns a nonprofit corporation, a board of directors controls the organization. The board is a group of volunteers whose responsibility it is to make sure the nonprofit adheres to its mission, safeguards its assets, and operates in the public interest.

NONPROFIT CORPORATIONS CAN MAKE A PROFIT

People assume that because nonprofit organizations are not created for financial gain they do not make a profit. This is not necessarily true.

Indeed, some nonprofits run a deficit every year. That is, their expenses exceed their income. But the most successful ones do earn a profit, which is often called surplus or net revenue. (I bet you didn't know that Harvard University is a nonprofit corporation, or that it currently has an endowment of over $25 billion.) Instead of being distributed to shareholders as is the case with for-profit corporations, the profits or surplus earned by nonprofits are used to accomplish the organization's mission. So it's not a matter of whether a nonprofit can make a profit, but what happens to the profits.

At the end of the day, nonprofits are in fact corporations, even if they're exempt from state and/or federal taxes.

BUSINESS JUST THE SAME

If this is the route you intend to take, don't think you can be lackadaisical simply because your organization is tax-exempt. Don't assume that government and corporate grants will flood your organization's coffers. They won't. Running your nonprofit will in many ways be no different than operating a for-profit. Many of the same rules and business protocols apply. You still have to market your programs and services so that people know they exist, that your organization exists. You still have to hire qualified employees, or passionate volunteers. You still have to pay business expenses.

Your best bet is to develop marketing plans, *in advance,* that are designed to raise monies from various sources, including: state, federal and corporate grants; fundraising activities; individual donations, and earnings from products sold or services rendered. The key is to not put all your eggs in one basket.

What About Lobbying?

Private foundations are not permitted to lobby. That is, they cannot engage in direct contact with legislators in an attempt to influence specific legislation. If they do, they'll risk losing their tax-exempt status.

Charities, on the other hand, *can* lobby but only to the extent that their lobbying activities do not become one of their primary activities. Plus they must report their lobbying expenditures to the IRS. Furthermore, charities are prohibited from participating in or trying to influence political campaigns. They may, however, engage in voter education activities during political campaigns.

Social welfare organizations (such as the NAACP) and trade associations don't have the same lobbying restrictions that charities are bound by. But there's a catch: they can't use funds from government grants or contracts for lobbying activities. It would be deemed a conflict of interest.

Incorporating Your Nonprofit Organization

In addition to the steps spelled out in Chapter 8, there are a few more things you'll need to do to properly incorporate your nonprofit organization.

As with a for-profit corporation, you should draft a comprehensive business plan for your nonprofit. Be sure to address the following issues:

- The organization's vision, mission and goals
- The nature and scope of the needs the organization will try to meet
- What activities the organization will take on to accomplish its mission
- What unique contribution your organization will make
- How your organization will finance its activities
- Who will serve on the board of director, as staff members, advisors and volunteers

Also, prepare and include proposed budgets for the first few years of operation.

Once you've done this, you should prepare the "Articles of Incorporation," bylaws and minutes of the first board meeting.

The articles of incorporation comprise the basic document by which your organization will be governed. It will establish the nonprofit's name and purpose, and any limitations on its activities. It will also contain a statement declaring the fact that your organization is a not-for-profit corporation, and will provide the address of the corporation, the names and addresses of the initial directors and a designation for the formal delivery of a writ, summons or other legal process. (This is often called service of process.)

The bylaws are more detailed than the articles of incorporation. They should spell out how your organization will operate: the election and appointment of officers and directors, the conduct of board meetings, the responsibilities of officers, the rights of members (if applicable), and so forth. Bylaws are adopted at the first meeting of the board of directors, which is usually held after filing the articles of incorporation.

Minutes of the first board meeting must be taken. They should include resolutions to adopt bylaws, elect officers, authorize the officers to apply for tax-exempt status, etc.

Applying for Tax-Exempt Status

Contrary to popular belief, a nonprofit organization is *not* automatically bestowed tax-exempt status. You must apply for this status both on the state and federal level. On the state level, you'll have to complete and submit the appropriate forms to the Dept. of Taxation and Finance. The IRS, in Washington, D.C., is the governing agency on the federal level. That's where you'll send your application and fees.

The form used is 1023, "Application for Recognition of Exemption," under section 501 (c) (3) of the Internal Revenue Code. Instructions come with the forms. You should get a response within two or three months.

Depending on the organization's *projected* income, you'll have to pay a fee of either $150 or $500. The fee, which must accompany your application, has to include Form 8718, "User Fee for Exempt Organization Determination Letter Request."

While you're at it, apply for your "Employer Identification Number" (EIN). This is accomplished by filling out and submitting form SS-4 to the IRS.

Annual information (or tax) returns, Form 990, must be filed by most tax-exempt organizations. They, too, come with instructions.

This stuff can get complicated, so it's advisable to retain a lawyer who specializes in forming nonprofit organizations. A good place to start is to contact your state's bar association (or a regional bar association) and ask them for a list of lawyers who specialize in forming nonprofit corporations. Or you might want to contact other nonprofits that are doing the work you intend to do, and ask them for guidance.

chapter 10

BEING YOUR OWN BOSS

I BET A *BIG* REASON you want to go into business is so you can be your own boss, set your own hours and call all the shots. That's all well and good, but keep in mind that initially you'll probably have to wear all the hats. You'll be the one to order supplies and equipment, to package merchandise, promote the business, keep the books, organize the records, answer customer inquiries, ship the goods, and so on.

As an entrepreneur, you have to be careful not to spread yourself too thin. At first, though, you'll probably have to multitask. You'll have to do whatever it takes to keep your business operational. But in the end you don't want to become a slave to your business any more than you want to be a slave to a job.

One way to make sure that doesn't happen is by hiring a competent staff. But knowing when and how to hire and retain *good* employees is not a simple task. It takes a bit of experience to be able to attract, employ and keep qualified workers.

How will you go about hiring the right employees for your business? What qualifications will potential employees have to meet? How much will you pay them? Will you offer employee benefits and/or incentives?

Advisors: One-on-One Counselors

Before hiring employees (even relatives or friends) it's a good idea to seek consultation on hiring, management and other related issues. The last thing you need while growing your business is to be penalized for breaking labor laws you didn't even know existed.

Two excellent *free* sources of business advice are SCORE (Service Corps of Retired Executives), an 11,000-member volunteer association sponsored by the Small Business Administration (SBA) that matches volunteer business-management counselors with clients in need of expert advice, and Small Business Development Centers (SBDC), which provide management and technical assistance to start-up and existing small businesses. These centers are strategically based on college campuses across the country, and bring together the resources of the university, the private sector and government.

There's a lot more stuff that ought to be considered as your business grows and you decide it's time to hire employees and delegate responsibilities.

The good thing is that you're not alone. There are people and organizations that want you to succeed. Why go it alone when you don't have to?

chapter 11

FLOODING THE MARKET

MAKE NO MISTAKE ABOUT it: your number one goal should be to find out what customers want and need, and then fill it. Money is secondary. If your customers aren't consistently satisfied, or if prospective customers don't even know that you exist, you won't be in business for long. Said another way, your business will only be as successful as your customers are loyal. It's that simple.

Before we get ahead of ourselves, let's be clear about what marketing is. Simply put, your target market is made up of the potential customers for your product or service. These are your ideal customers, the ones who are likely to buy your products or services.

Marketing, then, is your overall strategic plan to reach and satisfy your ideal customers' wants and needs. You can't simply have a product or service and hope that customers will come knocking on your doors — or hitting you up on your web site. It just doesn't work that way. You have to make your presence known.

Likewise, don't try to be all things to all customers. You'll end up missing your mark. Instead, carve out a niche, a segment of the overall market.

IDENTIFYING YOUR NICHE

Think of the overall market as a pie and a niche as your share (or slice) of the pie. There are a number of ways that you can effectively carve out your own niche. One strategy is to offer a product or service that no one else offers. My friend and mentor Steve Mariotti is fond of this approach. One of the ten things he believes all students of his entrepreneurship programs should know is: "Don't compete — create." Another method entails specializing in only one type of business or industry. And still another way to carve out your niche is to serve an unserved or underserved market, one where there's little or no competition.

MARKET RESEARCH

When it comes to your ideal customer you need to learn as much as you can about them: what motivates them, what makes them tick. That's what market research is all about: finding out who your potential customers are and understanding what they want and need.

Market research should not be an afterthought, something you decide to do *after* you've opened your doors for business. Like almost everything else in business, do your homework first. In this case, conduct market research *before* going into business.

Start with developing a customer profile. Where do your prospective customers live? Where do they shop? What is their age range and lifestyle? How much do they earn? What are their hobbies? Their spending habits? You get the idea. The more you know about your ideal customer, your target market, the easier it will be for you to reach and satisfy them.

One way to learn what prospective customers want is to ask them. Conduct face-to-face, telephone, mail or online interviews or surveys. This approach can save you a lot of time and money that might otherwise be invested in a product or service that very few people want or need.

Another source of market research is the Internet. With a Google search you're only a few key words away from finding out pretty much anything you want to know. Even if you don't have direct access to the Internet make it your business to take advantage of the computers at your local public or business library. Or encourage your loved ones to do so. State and federal agencies, such as the U.S. Department of Commerce, are yet another helpful source of market research. They compile and make available (either for free or a nominal fee) a vast amount of statistical research that will help you identify demographics as well as market, economic and industry trends.

Finally, trade associations collect industry-specific information that you can use to get a feel for a market's size, demographics and trends. A good library will have directories containing the names, descriptions and contact information of thousands upon thousands of trade associations.

WHY SHOULD CUSTOMERS DO BUSINESS WITH YOU ANYWAY?

This is the million-dollar question. And you'd better have the correct answer.

You have to stand out in your customers' or prospective customers' minds. If you don't give them a reason to do business with you, they won't! From the jump, you need to know what you can do better than the competition. What is your unique selling proposition (USP), your competitive advantage? If you can't answer this question, stop while you're ahead. Seriously. Do not go into business if you are unable to articulate why customers will turn their hard-earned money over to you instead of to your competition. Remember, this is a business, not a hobby. Customers want to know how they will benefit from doing business with you. They want to know how your products or services will benefit them. They won't spend money simply because they think you're a nice person.

In order to stay in business *and* increase your share of the market, your competitive advantage must be sustainable. It must involve an ongoing, long-term strategy.

THE 4 PS

The basis of all marketing begins with the 4 Ps of marketing: product (or service), place, price and promotion. Collectively these elements are known as the *marketing mix.*

Think of them as the necessary ingredients to effectively and efficiently launch a product or service and execute vigorous marketing campaigns. No one element or ingredient is more important than another; each will play a necessary role in your overall marketing program.

Here's how the factors relate to one another and how they pertain to your business.

Product

Let's say you plan to self-publish young adult urban fiction that contains positive and uplifting messages. (By the way, this genre is off the hook at the moment.) Your published books would be your product, the first ingredient to go into your marketing mix. And though no one ingredient is more important than any other, without a product (or service) to sell you have no business — just an idea.

Place

Whether you intend to sell your books at flea markets, shopping malls, college centers or elsewhere will be predicated on several things. First, are *your* customers/readers likely to be at these places in large enough numbers to justify the costs associated with setting up shop? Secondly, if you plan to run your business from home are there any zoning regulations that might prevent you from doing so?

Price

You don't have a lot of flexibility when it comes to setting an "appropriate" price for your young adult urban fiction. This is because there's pretty much a *standard* price range for this genre of books; they usually sell for between $12.95 and $15. Even so, pricing your products (books) is an important consideration. If you charge too much people won't buy your books; charge too little and you'll have a difficult time breaking even. In the end, pricing is based on what your customers — not you — think your products are worth.

Promotion

The bottom line is that if you do not promote your books, if you don't announce to the world that your books even exist, then guess what: only you and a few other people will know about your novel. By failing to zealously promote your novel you guarantee its short life and ignoble demise.

Generally speaking there's a clear distinction between promotion and advertising (the difference is explained under the next subheading), but for purposes of the 4 Ps promotion is meant to encompass both.

Never stop marketing! Don't ever rest on your laurels. Always try to stay ahead of the competition. By regularly conducting a competitive analysis (first, before you go into business, then at predetermined intervals), a comparison between your company and your competitors, you'll have a clearer picture of what's going on in the market and industry. You'll be aware of how well the competition is doing. Accordingly, you may decide to either step up your competitive advantage or change your tactics altogether.

ADVERTISING VERSUS PROMOTIONS

You have to consistently make people aware of your business *and* the benefits of your products or services. Four ways of doing this are:

- *Personal contact* (in person, by telephone, etc.)
- *Through others* (word of mouth, referrals, public relations)
- *Written communication* (ads, brochures, newsletters, etc.)
- *Demonstrations* (product samples, web sites, etc.)

Personal contact, written communication and demonstrations are all variations of *direct* marketing.

Marketing activities can be divided into two categories: Advertising and Promotions. Advertising is what comes to mind when most people think of marketing. But advertising is only one aspect of marketing.

Based on your analysis of the market (and how much you can afford), you'll determine whether advertising over the radio, on TV, or in print is the best route to go. Your advertising must be specifically targeted. If your customers read the Yellow Pages, then that's where you should advertise. Likewise, if they spend a lot of time on the Internet you'd do well to either place banner ads on other Web sites or your own Web site or e-commerce site.

Advertising can be quite expensive. It's not for every budget, especially most small- or medium-size businesses. A one-column inch, (5 pt.) black and white classified ad in The New York Times will set you back $595, while a one-time display ad (1" x 2.25") in Entrepreneur magazine costs $795. A radio slot on, say, 98.7 KISS FM, a popular R & B radio station in New York City, will cost you $300 for thirty seconds, and that's for a weekend slot. A weekday slot during popular segments will set you back $1,200.

To put these costs in perspective, let's say you wrote and self-published a memoir about your prison experiences. The book retails for $15. At the current "Small Press" rate (1.875" x 1") of $595, you'd have to sell a minimum of 40 books in order to get your money back (break even) with an ad in The New York Times. Likewise, just to break even, your ad in Entrepreneur magazine would have to sell 53 books, while your radio ad would require 20 book sales (80 books during popular program segments).

When it comes to advertising, it's important that you think, first, in terms of at least breaking even. Give a lot of forethought to the most suitable venues or publications to advertise in. After all, you don't have money to burn.

A cheaper route would be for you to draft and distribute a press release in the hope that you'd get a free mention on radio, in a newspaper or magazine or space on someone else's Web site. All it'll cost is a stamp to mail the press release. Or if you fax or e-mail it, it won't cost you anything.

Promotions is another, less expensive, method of attracting customers and increasing sales. There are all kinds of ways to promote your business, from passing out business cards to giving free or paid speeches and/or seminars.

If there's one thing people in the drug game do effectively it's promote, promote, promote. Whether it's by word of mouth; compensating customers and prospective customers for referring others; buy-3-get-1-free gimmicks; "happy hours;" or the size, color or shape of packaging, drug peddlers know how to get the word out about their "business" and its "product." Take a page from their playbook (but just this page!) by coming up with creative ways to promote your business.

Print fliers and circulars, sponsor community events, volunteer your time to specific groups or organizations tied to your market, offer incentives, promote giveaways and put on contests. These are all inexpensive ways of publicizing your business. You might also want to create a company newsletter. It can be a page or two, and it doesn't have to be paper-based. Instead, you can create an e-newsletter (electronic newsletter), one that's distributed by e-mail or fax.

Consider printing your company's logo, with or without an accompanying message, on t-shirts. Those who wear them will become walking advertisements.

Whenever you have something newsworthy to say about your business, such as the launch of a new product or expansion to another market or region, write a press release and send it to targeted newspapers, magazines, broadcast outlets or Internet sites.

Keep people saying good things about your company and its products. Join trade associations, clubs and other organizations that might put you in touch with potential customers. Get out there and mingle. In business being bashful and unassertive could be a liability.

Always ask customers to refer others to you. This word-of-mouth buzz is basically a free endorsement of your company and its products or services. Not only are referrals less expensive than other kinds of marketing, but referred customers come with their wallets open. They're ready to spend — now. Always provide incentives for referrals, and always show your appreciation.

PART 3
MONEY MATTERS

chapter 12

CASH RULES

MONEY IS THE LIFEBLOOD of any business. Without sufficient positive cash flow, you won't be in business for long. Grand ideas and genius-inspired products or services won't be of much use if they can't help your business bring in enough money to keep it afloat and growing. Bottom line: cash rules.

SOURCES OF BUSINESS FINANCING

Two of the more common sources of business financing are personal savings and people you know.

Personal savings

According to the Small Business Administration, personal savings are by far the primary source of business financing. Indeed, 57 percent of entrepreneurs jumpstart their business by either tapping into their bank accounts, using their credit cards, an inheritance or life insurance policies, or taking out a second mortgage or a home equity line of credit. Whatever it takes.

Your options are much more limited, of course. Chances are you don't own your own home (at least not yet), so borrowing against the value or equity in a home is out of the question. But if you heed my advice in Chapter 3, "About Them Benjamins," to save and invest *while* you're still in prison, and in Chapter 14, "Credit Matters," on how to establish good credit, you'll be ahead of the pack when it comes to having access to business start-up capital.

Relatives and friends

This is another common source of funding. Since they already know you, relatives and friends will more readily try to support your efforts. Of course, there will be naysayers, but we're not talking about them. Let them sulk on the sidelines while you live out your dreams.

Business startup monies that you receive from relatives or friends can come in the form of a gift, loan or investment. A gift, well...is a gift. You don't have to repay it. With a loan, which is a debt, you are obligated to reimburse whomever loaned you money, with interest. Or the loan might be interest-free, where you'd only have to pay back the principal.

No matter the type of loan, it's a mistake to think that since it's a loved one or friend who's lending you money, a handshake agreement will suffice. Friend or no friend, relative or not, any loan obligation that you take on should be put in writing. It should be treated as any other business relationship. This will reduce or eliminate the possibility of future misunderstandings or disputes. Even more important, having a written loan contract can preserve your familial or friendship bonds.

An investment (or equity stake) is a whole different animal. Instead of loaning you money with the understanding that your association will end once they get their principal back plus interest, investors have an equity, or ownership, stake and expect the alliance to last longer. At least until they're able to sell their share in the business for a satisfactory return on their investment.

Business loans

Most banks and other lending institutions are very reluctant to fork over money to business start-ups. They want your business to have a track record so they can better determine if you'd make a good loan risk.

As is pointed out in Chapter 13, "Bank On It," banks are in business to make money. Like any other business, their principal concern is the bottom line — profits. Your job is to demonstrate that you're a good loan risk, and that you have the character, collateral (yes, they want collateral) and capacity (or ability) to repay the loan — with interest.

Depending on your business's needs, what stage of the business cycle it's in and your track record, various short- , intermediate and long-term bank loans may be available.

Short-term loans:

A *line of credit* is a specific sum set aside in a bank for a company to use as needed. The set term of the line of credit can be as short as thirty days or as long as two years. It all depends on expected revenues. Interest on these types of loans is computed only on the amount actually taken out, but a commitment fee of ½% or 1% of the total credit line is usually imposed, to compensate the bank for reserving funds that may not be used.

Inventory loans are sometimes considered safer bets for banks lending money to small businesses. Instead of simply extending a line of credit, a bank may be more open to lending you money if inventory in your business is used as collateral. Funds are made available, as needed, and as inventory is sold and accounts receivables are satisfied.

Commercial loans are repaid in a lump sum at the end of the term, usually three to six months. With these types of loans banks are mostly concerned about a company's credit rating and its source of repayment.

Accounts receivable financing essentially converts unpaid accounts (receivables) into quick cash. Specifically, these are accounts that are less than 60 days past due. With this kind of financing, your customers must themselves be deemed creditworthy.

Banks will ordinarily advance 60% to 80% of the face value of the receivables. This amount is repayable as your customers' checks come in. And as you receive the checks, you'll be required to pass them on to the bank. The bank then takes its predetermined percentage and deposits the rest in your account, charging interest only on the amount outstanding. Accounts receivable financing allows banks to get their money back — with interest, of course — in installments, and helps with your business's cash flow.

This short-term financing arrangement usually has a one-year term, but many banks are flexible, so a revolving format may be available to allow more time to repay the loan.

Factoring is similar to accounts receivable financing. But in this case the bank (or a factoring company) actually buys your accounts receivable outright, instead of simply lending you money against collateralized receivables. And also unlike accounts receivables financing, with factoring customers make payments directly to the bank or factoring company, not to you. The bank takes on credit risks and assumes the responsibilities of collecting receivables.

Since this type of financing is more risky from a banker's perspective, receivables are subject to more analysis before they are purchased, to reduce the number of poor risks. Factoring, for obvious reasons, will cost you more than most other forms of short-term loans.

Intermediate and long-term loans:

Term loans are intermediate loans (one to five years) that are usually used to finance equipment and machinery. While the bank may not view the asset you're purchasing as collateral, it will expect the asset to serve as the source for generating increased sales. Repayment schedules are typically on a quarterly basis, with principal payments remaining constant while interest, calculated on the amount outstanding, decreases over the term of the loan.

Real estate loans allow you to finance expansion by borrowing against the value of real estate you already own.

Commercial and industrial mortgages may suit you if you get the chance to buy the building you are leasing. Ordinarily, a bank will loan you up to 75% of the appraised value of the property. And while a 20- or 25-year mortgage would certainly lower your monthly installments, chances are the bank will instead offer you a 5- or 10-year mortgage. Your monthly payments, however, will probably be pegged to a 15- or 20-year amortization period. When the mortgage comes due, you'll have to pay the full amount that is owed in what is called a "balloon" payment.

Personal loans are secured by your personal assets. For obvious reasons, many bankers prefer personal loans. Examples of the kinds of personal assets that might be used as collateral are cash, savings or checking accounts, certificates of deposit, money market accounts and money market funds, stocks, bonds and mutual funds, as well as your home mortgage. But putting a lien or second mortgage on your home can be very risky. You could not only lose your business, but the roof over your head.

Writing a loan proposal

Assuming you've already written a business plan, preparing a loan proposal shouldn't be too difficult. The proposal can be organized into eight sections.

Summary: This section consists of your name and title, your company's name and address, the type of business it is, the purpose of the business, how much money you're asking for, and how you intend to repay the loan. (Refer to the "Executive Summary" section in your business plan.)

Management Profile: Just as important (to bankers, that is,) as the amount of money you're asking for and the sources of repayment is who's actually running your business. After all, businesses don't run themselves, people run them. Having an experienced management team in place will make your loan proposal process that much easier.

Write a paragraph or two on each of your top-management personnel. Include information about background, education, experience, skills, accomplishments and areas of expertise. (You should already have this information in the "Management" section of your business plan.)

Business description: Just like in your business plan's "Business Description" section, this part of your loan proposal should contain your company's legal structure, age, number of employees, a brief description of the products or services you sell, the size and trends of your market and industry, as well as a competitive analysis. The bank's loan officer might also want to know the value of any inventory you have in stock, plus its turnover rate and marketability. Finally, if you currently have accounts receivable or accounts payable, be sure to mention it. This information will paint a clearer picture of your business's financial standing.

Projections: Explain what growth opportunities exist in your industry and how you intend to exploit them over the next year and the next five years. Spell out a realistic timetable for achieving your goals.

Financial statements: You'll need to produce past (going back three years) and current balance sheets and income statements, as well as two sets of projected balance sheets, income statements and cash-flow statements (one based on receiving the loan, the other on going forward without it). Your projections must be realistic.

The loan process doesn't end with your business's financial statements. Bankers will check your personal credit rating, along with your company's. They'll expect you to submit personal financial statements with your loan proposal, including tax returns for the past three years.

Purpose of the loan: What will the money be used for? Be specific.

Amount of the loan request: Don't make up just any figure. Do your homework. Draw up a list of things that you need money for, and quote exactly how much you need for each line item. Support your calculations with previous years' cost figures and estimates from suppliers, if applicable.

Repayment Plan: This is the $99,000 question. You had better have two different sources of repayment, one of them being the asset you're trying to secure financing for. If the asset will not increase sales, it must either cut costs or improve overall efficiency. Otherwise, why would you need it? Also keep in mind that any asset you hope to finance must last at least as long as the term of the loan.

Other Lenders

Angel investors are high-net-worth private investors. These individuals have assets in excess of $1,000,000 and, for a number of reasons, like to invest in start-ups.

Angel investors typically expect a return of 1,000% or ten times their investment.

Venture capitalists are similar to angel investors in that a high (roughly six times, or 600%) return on investment is expected. But unlike angel investors, venture capitalists (or investment companies) almost always want an equity or ownership stake in return for the cash they put up. And they'll want to sit on your board of directors or advisors. In other words, they'll want some say in how your business is run.

Venture capitalists often hope that your business will one day go public. This is how many of them make their high return on investment.

Micro-credit: These are very small business loans — for as little as $500 — that a number of nonprofit organizations and the SBA offer.

chapter 13

BANK ON IT

Deciding Who to Bank With

ALL BANKS ARE NOT created equally. Each offers its own variety of services, each has distinct polices, and no two banks are in the same financial standing. (You can find out the footing of most banks by getting a report from Veribank.)

Don't automatically assume that the community bank where you keep your personal bank account is the right bank to do business with. Shop around for a bank (or banks) that offers programs for small businesses and that will accommodate your specific needs.

Compare the various types of savings, checking and money market accounts. Do they charge for each check deposited? If so, how much? Do they pay interest on business checking accounts? If so, what is the minimum balance required? How often will interest earned on your accounts be credited or posted (daily, quarterly or semi-annually)? Do they offer online banking? If so, can you set up an account? And what fees will you incur? What is their record of making loans to small businesses?

Choosing a banking partner does not have to be tedious. But you should give some forethought to your business's banking needs and goals.

In using the term *bank*, I am also referring to credit unions and savings and loans (S&Ls), otherwise known as thrifts. These financial institutions offer basically the same types of accounts and services and have similar interest rates and fee schedules.

Remember, banks are in business to make money. They're not a charity. You are doing *them* a favor by depositing your money with them. One way that banks make money is by charging more interest on various types of loans than the amount of interest they have to pay out to depositors. Another source of revenues comes from the laundry list of fees charged for myriad services. Finally, banks invest in everything from real estate and marketable securities to precious metals and private companies.

In the end, their goal is the same: to minimize risk while they maximize their return on investment (ROI).

Befriending Your Banker

When it comes to banking, think in terms of establishing, maintaining, and nurturing long-term relationships. Consider your banker, especially loan officers, your business partner. Make it your business to keep her up to date on the status of your business. Every time you make deposits or withdrawals in person you should say a few words to her about your business. Mind you, I'm not talking about seeking a loan. At least not yet. The purpose of discussing your business, market trends and the industry that you're in is to demonstrate to your loan officer that you are on top of your business, and that you consider her a partner. It telegraphs that you value your relationship with her. As a result, she will be more inclined to provide you with information about available money sources, potential partnerships and other business opportunities. Loan officers serve as your ears to the ground. They have access to a wealth of market intelligence.

chapter 14

CREDIT MATTERS

ESTABLISHING GOOD CREDIT IS one of the most important things you can do, for personal and business reasons. Your credit report and credit score (more on both later) will determine the interest rate you'll be charged for such things as business loans, car loans, insurance premiums and mortgage loans. In fact, your score will factor into whether you receive a loan at all.

The word credit derives from the Latin word *credere,* which means to trust, entrust or believe. That's what is meant by creditworthiness. Creditors and lenders want to know if they can entrust you with *their* money. They need to know if they should believe that you will honor your debt obligations.

Surely you didn't think credit meant free money. It doesn't. When creditors extend credit they are essentially loaning money on a short-term basis. (It becomes a long-term *loan* if you do not pay it back on time.)

Before we get into how you can build or re-establish good credit, even if you've never had credit or a bank loan, let's go over the three C's of credit and the four types of credit cards.

THREE C'S OF CREDIT

- *Capacity* is your ability to repay the principal borrowed *with* interest. To determine this, the amount of your salary or wages is taken into consideration, as is the value of any assets you own and debt commitments you owe.

- *Character* refers to your credibility or creditworthiness in the eyes of potential creditors, employers or landlords. It is evaluated by examining your credit history, record of past payments and delinquent payments, and the length of time at your current job and home.

- *Collateral* is anything of value that can be used as security. Some creditors require collateral in case you're unable to satisfy your debt obligations.

FOUR TYPES OF CREDIT CARDS

All credit cards are not the same. Some are issued by banks or other financial institutions. Others are issued by retail stores or large corporations. Most credit cards offer revolving credit. This means you can pay off the outstanding or current balance in monthly installments. Charge cards, on the other hand, require that you pay off the full balance each month. Penalties are incurred if you do not pay the entire balance during the next billing cycle. Ultimately you could lose the "privilege" of owning and using the card.

Here are examples of each type of card:

Bank	Retail	Charge	Secured
Visa	Eddie Bauer	American Express	(Same as
Mastercard	Macy's	Diners Club	bank card)

Of the four types of credit cards, retail cards like Sears or J.C. Penny's and secured credit cards charge the highest interest rates, sometimes as high as twenty percent per year.

Secured credit cards are ideal for formerly incarcerated people because almost all secured card issuers accept people who have no credit history, or poor credit.

In addition to comparing interest rates and when you're expected to pay the balance on your credit cards, you should read the fine print before choosing a credit card issuer. What are their annual percent rates (APR)? This is the amount of interest you will pay on your balance. Is there an application fee or annual fees? If so, how much are they? Application fees are also called account set-up or membership fees. Watch out for these; they can be as much as $250. Some cards, and almost all secured credit cards, have annual fees. Basically these are charged for the privilege of holding a credit card.

Other fees to look out for and avoid are late fees and over-the-limit fees. If a monthly payment is received by the creditor after the grace period (the time between the close of the billing cycle and the payment due date — usually 20 days) elapses, you'll be charged a late fee of up to $35. As long as you pay off the full balance due within the grace period (no later than the payment due date) you will owe no interest. But if you only pay some of the balance due — *even if* within the grace period — you will be charged interest on the outstanding balance due. And if you go over the card's credit limit (more about this later) you'll be charged an over-the-limit fee every month until you bring your balance under the limit. Some secured credit cards have *no* grace period. This means that you'll have to pay interest on all purchases from the day they are made.

What Is a Secured Credit Card and How Do They Work?

A secured credit card is a bank card that is backed (or secured) by money that you deposit and keep in the bank. In effect, your bank account serves as security for the card. It represents collateral. The account is frozen while you have the card. If you don't pay your credit card bill, your bank deposit may be used to cover the debt.

As with any other type of bank account, you should comparison shop. Some secured credit card issuers pay interest (up to 4.5%) on the collateralized or frozen part of the account. Others don't, unless the size of the account exceeds a predetermined amount.

Whether you think it's fair or not, it takes credit to get credit. And since most incarcerated (and formerly incarcerated) persons have never owned a credit card or received a loan from a bank or finance company, starting off with a secured credit card and then graduating to an unsecured card is the best way to build a good credit record.

After six to twelve months of on-time payments, you'll probably begin to get offers from unsecured credit card issuers.

A big plus with owning a secured credit card is that they resemble and are used like unsecured credit cards. That is, they bear the Mastercard or Visa logo, and so to creditors they are just credit cards.

Hundreds of financial institutions offer secured credit cards.

What About Your Credit Limit?

Your credit limit is the maximum amount you are allowed to borrow, or charge, using your credit card. Most secured credit cards allow you to charge up to 100 % of the amount that is frozen on deposit. Others will grant only a percentage of the amount on deposit, while still others offer credit lines (another term for credit limit, or the maximum amount you can charge) of double the amount you have on deposit. The latter type is essentially a hybrid or mixed account; part of the account is secured and the other part is unsecured.

What You Will Need When Applying
For a Secured Credit Card

Obviously you will need money to deposit in a savings account. You'll also need to provide your social security number, proof of income, your home phone number, your address and verification of employment.

What Is a Credit Report and What Does It Contain?

A credit report is a record of your credit accounts: it shows the types of credit in use, your payment history, the length of credit history, maximum credit lines and current balance information. This information helps prospective lenders access your creditworthiness.

It helps them determine whether you are a good risk.

Who Compiles This Information?

Credit bureaus receive regular reports on your patterns of paying off — or not paying off — your debt obligations from companies that extend consumer credit. The bureaus then repackage this data and sell it to lenders who want to screen applicants. They're now available free of charge. The three largest credit reporting bureaus are Equifax, Transunion and Experian.

Following is how a typical credit report might look:

experian®

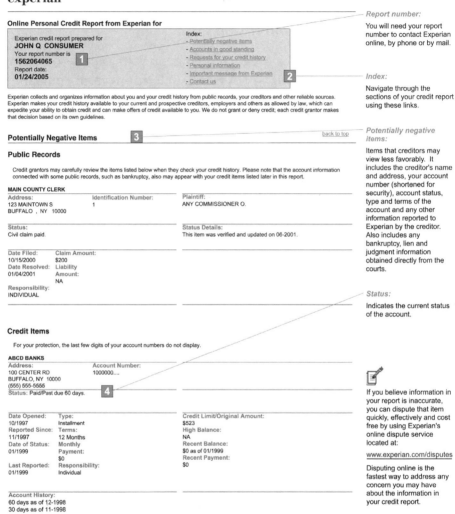

Online Personal Credit Report from Experian for

Experian credit report prepared for
JOHN Q CONSUMER
Your report number is
1562064065
Report date:
01/24/2005

Index:
- Potentially negative items
- Accounts in good standing
- Requests for your credit history
- Personal information
- Important message from Experian
- Contact us

Experian collects and organizes information about you and your credit history from public records, your creditors and other reliable sources. Experian makes your credit history available to your current and prospective creditors, employers and others as allowed by law, which can expedite your ability to obtain credit and can make offers of credit available to you. We do not grant or deny credit; each credit grantor makes that decision based on its own guidelines.

Potentially Negative Items

back to top

Public Records

Credit grantors may carefully review the items listed below when they check your credit history. Please note that the account information connected with some public records, such as bankruptcy, also may appear with your credit items listed later in this report.

MAIN COUNTY CLERK

Address:	Identification Number:	Plaintiff:
123 MAINTOWN S	1	ANY COMMISSIONER O.
BUFFALO , NY 10000		

Status:	Status Details:
Civil claim paid.	This item was verified and updated on 06-2001.

Date Filed:	Claim Amount:
10/15/2000	$200
Date Resolved:	Liability
01/04/2001	Amount:
	NA
Responsibility:	
INDIVIDUAL	

Credit Items

For your protection, the last few digits of your account numbers do not display.

ABCD BANKS

Address:	Account Number:
100 CENTER RD	1000000....
BUFFALO, NY 10000	
(555) 555-5555	

Status: Paid/Past due 60 days.

Date Opened:	Type:	Credit Limit/Original Amount:
10/1997	Installment	$523
Reported Since:	Terms:	High Balance:
11/1997	12 Months	NA
Date of Status:	Monthly	Recent Balance:
01/1999	Payment:	$0 as of 01/1999
	$0	Recent Payment:
Last Reported:	Responsibility:	$0
01/1999	Individual	

Account History:
60 days as of 12-1998
30 days as of 11-1998

Report number:

You will need your report number to contact Experian online, by phone or by mail.

Index:

Navigate through the sections of your credit report using these links.

Potentially negative items:

Items that creditors may view less favorably. It includes the creditor's name and address, your account number (shortened for security), account status, type and terms of the account and any other information reported to Experian by the creditor. Also includes any bankruptcy, lien and judgment information obtained directly from the courts.

Status:

Indicates the current status of the account.

If you believe information in your report is inaccurate, you can dispute that item quickly, effectively and cost free by using Experian's online dispute service located at:

www.experian.com/disputes

Disputing online is the fastest way to address any concern you may have about the information in your credit report.

MAIN COLL AGENCIES

Address:	Account Number:	Original Creditor:
PO BOX 123	0123456789	TELEVISE CABLE COMM.
ANYTOWN, PA 10000		
(555) 555-5555		

Status: Collection account. $95 past due as of 4-2000.

Date Opened:	Type:	Credit Limit/Original Amount:
01/2000	Installment	$95
Reported Since:	Terms:	High Balance:
04/2000	NA	NA
Date of Status:	Monthly	Recent Balance:
04/2000	Payment:	$95 as of 04/2000
	$0	Recent Payment:
Last Reported:	Responsibility:	$0
04/2000	Individual	

Your statement: ITEM DISPUTED BY CONSUMER

Account History:
Collection as of 4-2000

Accounts in Good Standing `5`

back to top

AUTOMOBILE AUTO FINANCE

Address:	Account Number:
100 MAIN ST E	12345678998....
SMALLTOWN, MD 90001	
(555) 555-5555	

Status: Open/Never late.

Date Opened:	Type: `6`	Credit Limit/Original Amount:
01/2000	Installment	$10,355
Reported Since:	Terms:	High Balance:
01/2000	65 Months	NA
Date of Status:	Monthly	Recent Balance:
08/2001	Payment:	$7,984 as of 08/2001
	$210	Recent Payment:
Last Reported:	Responsibility:	$0
08/2001	Individual	

MAIN

Address:	Account Number:
PO BOX 1234	1234567899876
FORT LAUDERDALE, FL 10009	

Status: Closed/Never late.

Date Opened:	Type:	Credit Limit/Original Amount:
03/1991	Revolving	NA
Reported Since:	Terms:	High Balance:
03/1991	1 Months	$3,228
Date of Status:	Monthly	Recent Balance:
08/2000	Payment:	$0 /paid as of 08/2000
	$0	Recent Payment:
Last Reported:	Responsibility:	$0
08/2000	Individual	

Your statement:
Account closed at consumer's request

Accounts in good standing:

Lists accounts that ha
positive status and m
viewed favorably by
creditors. Some cred
do not report to us, s
of your accounts may
listed.

Type:

Account type indicate
whether your account
revolving or an install
account.

Requests for Your Credit History

back to top

Requests Viewed By Others

We make your credit history available to your current and prospective creditors and employers as allowed by law. Personal data about you may be made available to companies whose products and services may interest you.

The section below lists all who have requested in the recent past to review your credit history as a result of actions involving you, such as the completion of a credit application or the transfer of an account to a collection agency, mortgage or loan application, etc. Creditors may view these requests when evaluating your creditworthiness.

HOMESALE REALTY CO

Address:	Date of Request:
2000 S MAINROAD BLVD STE	07/16/2001
ANYTOWN CA 11111	
(555) 555-5555	

Comments:
Real estate loan on behalf of 1000 COPRORATE COMPANY. This inquiry is scheduled to continue on record until 8-2003.

ABC BANK

Address:	Date of Request:
PO BOX 100	02/23/2001
BUFFALO NY 10000	
(555) 555-5555	

Comments:
Permissible purpose. This inquiry is scheduled to continue on record until 3-2003.

ANYTOWN FUNDING INC

Address:	Date of Request:
100 W MAIN AVE STE 100	07/25/2000
INTOWN CA 10000	
(555) 555-5555	

Comments:
Permissible purpose. This inquiry is scheduled to continue on record until 8-2002.

Requests Viewed Only By You

The section below lists all who have a permissible purpose by law and have requested in the recent past to review your information. You may not have initiated these requests, so you may not recognize each source. We offer information about you to those with a permissible purpose, for example, to:

- other creditors who want to offer you preapproved credit;
- an employer who wishes to extend an offer of employment;
- a potential investor in assessing the risk of a current obligation;
- Experian or other credit reporting agencies to process a report for you;
- your existing creditors to monitor your credit activity (date listed may reflect only the most recent request).

We report these requests **only to you** as a record of activities. We **do not** provide this information to other creditors who evaluate your creditworthiness.

MAIN BANK USA

Address:	Date of Request:
1 MAIN CTR AA 11	08/10/2001
BUFFALO NY 10000	

MAINTOWN BANK

Address:	Date of Request:
PO BOX 100	08/05/2001
MAINTOWNS DE 10000	
(555) 555-5555	

ANYTOWN DATA CORPS

Address:	Date of Request:
2000 S MAINTOWN BLVD STE	07/16/2001
INTOWN CO 11111	
(555) 555-5555	

Requests for your credit history:

Also called "inquiries", requests for your credit history are logged on your report whenever anyone reviews your credit information. There are two types of inquiries.

Requests viewed by others

Inquiries resulting from a transaction initiated by you. These include inquiries from your applications for credit, housing or other loans. They also include transfer of an account to a collection agency. Creditors may view these items when evaluating your creditworthiness.

Requests viewed only by you

Inquiries resulting from transactions you may not have initiated but that are allowed under the FCRA. These include preapproved offers, as well as for employment, investment review, account monitoring by existing creditors, and requests by you for your own report. These items are shown only to you and have no impact on your creditworthiness or risk scores.

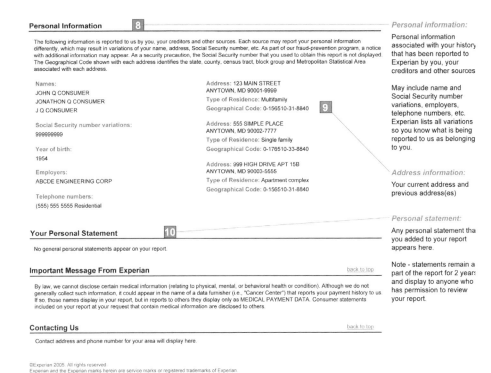

Personal Information 8

The following information is reported to us by you, your creditors and other sources. Each source may report your personal information differently, which may result in variations of your name, address, Social Security number, etc. As part of our fraud-prevention program, a notice with additional information may appear. As a security precaution, the Social Security number that you used to obtain this report is not displayed. The Geographical Code shown with each address identifies the state, county, census tract, block group and Metropolitan Statistical Area associated with each address.

Names:
JOHN Q CONSUMER
JONATHON Q CONSUMER
J Q CONSUMER

Social Security number variations:
999999999

Year of birth:
1954

Employers:
ABCDE ENGINEERING CORP

Telephone numbers:
(555) 555 5555 Residential

Address: 123 MAIN STREET
ANYTOWN, MD 90001-9999
Type of Residence: Multifamily
Geographical Code: 0-156510-31-8840 9

Address: 555 SIMPLE PLACE
ANYTOWN, MD 90002-7777
Type of Residence: Single family
Geographical Code: 0-176510-33-8840

Address: 999 HIGH DRIVE APT 15B
ANYTOWN, MD 90003-5555
Type of Residence: Apartment complex
Geographical Code: 0-156510-31-8840

Personal information:

Personal information associated with your history that has been reported to Experian by you, your creditors and other sources

May include name and Social Security number variations, employers, telephone numbers, etc. Experian lists all variations so you know what is being reported to us as belonging to you.

Address information:

Your current address and previous address(es)

Your Personal Statement 10

No general personal statements appear on your report.

Personal statement:

Any personal statement that you added to your report appears here.

Important Message From Experian   back to top

By law, we cannot disclose certain medical information (relating to physical, mental, or behavioral health or condition). Although we do not generally collect such information, it could appear in the name of a data furnisher (i.e., "Cancer Center") that reports your payment history to us. If so, those names display in your report, but in reports to others they display only as MEDICAL PAYMENT DATA. Consumer statements included on your report at your request that contain medical information are disclosed to others.

Note - statements remain a part of the report for 2 years and display to anyone who has permission to review your report.

Contacting Us   back to top

Contact address and phone number for your area will display here.

©Experian 2005. All rights reserved.
Experian and the Experian marks herein are service marks or registered trademarks of Experian

What Is Your Credit Score and How Can You Find Out What It Is?

As a way to quantify your credit behavior, and thus gauge your risk to lenders, a number of companies, each with their own scoring models, offer what's considered a snapshot of your credit risk.

The most well-known credit-scoring business is Fair, Isaac and Company. This is where the term "FICO Score" or "credit score" comes from.

These numerical scores range from 300 to 850, with the low end indicating a poor credit risk. A score of 620 is often considered the "cutoff point." Below that number you're likely to pay higher rates on loans. And if you have a very low score you probably will be denied a loan altogether.

You can buy a copy of your credit score from any one of the three largest credit reporting agencies or from *myfico.com*, the web site of Fair, Isaac and Co.

Recently, these three agencies announced that they'll work together to launch a new score called *Vantage Score*. The stated purpose of their collaboration is to address the issue of the different formulas that each agency has used to compute their scores.

Similar to grades in school, here's how your scores would stack up:

Score	Grade	Credit Outlook
901-990	A	Excellent rating; low interest rate
801-900	B	Good rating but short of excellent
701-800	C	Fair; moderate risk
601-700	D	Higher risk means higher interest rate
501-600	E	Highest risk; may not qualify for loan

Sources: Equifax, Experian, Transunion, AP

Repairing Credit Errors

Credit reporting agencies are prone to making errors. And identity fraud is on the rise. It's not uncommon for someone on the outside to use (and abuse) your name and social security number to purchase products and services. That's why getting and reviewing your credit report is so important. It's crucial that you get a copy of your credit report from each of the three largest credit reporting agencies at least once a year. Order a free report from www.annualcreditreport.com.

A low credit score, as was explained earlier, can affect whether you're extended credit and, if so, what interest rate you'll end up paying.

The Fair Credit Billing Act (15 USC 1692) is a federal law that protects you from billing errors and unauthorized charges. It gives you the right to ask a card issuer to remove and investigate any charges that you dispute.

In order to properly contest errors on a creditor's statement you have to write the credit card issuer within 60 days of the date of the statement in which the errors appeared. From that point the company cannot try to collect the disputed amount or report your account delinquent because of the error.

The company has 30 days to acknowledge your dispute and another 90 days to correct the error or explain why it believes the charge is valid.

You don't have to pay interest on the disputed charge, *if* it is settled in your favor. If, on the other hand, the dispute is settled in the creditor's or lender's favor, you will have to pay the disputed amount *plus* interest that has accrued.

chapter 15

KEEPING TRACK OF YOUR MONEY

PERHAPS MATH WAS ONE of your least favorite subjects in school. O.K., it was your worst. No matter, if you plan to be a successful entrepreneur there's no way around math. In the end, it's all about the numbers.

In Chapter 6, "Why Businesses Fail," I pointed out that one of the underlying reasons that businesses fail is poor cash-flow management. This chapter will help you avoid this common and costly mistake.

Whether you do it yourself, hire someone else to do it, or outsource the task, a bookkeeping system, one that tracks money coming into and flowing out of your business, must be put in place. You want to be able to keep track of every transaction that takes place: every sale, purchase, expense and the like. You'll need to be able to identify the various sources of income (or revenue) and expenses. This information will help you to reallocate resources when necessary and better manage your time and efforts.

In short, maintaining good financial records will keep you in touch with the day-to-day operations of your business. As a result, you'll more readily detect changes in customers' wants and needs, the seasonal ebbs and flows of your business, and whether your marketing strategies are effective.

Another important reason to maintain accurate and relevant

(meaning only what is necessary for *your* business) records is so that when tax time comes around, you won't have to go scrambling to sort out your records. You'll want to be organized and efficient. The last thing you want to happen is for the IRS to come knocking on your door for a field audit because of accounting irregularities. But if they do come, you'll want to at least have your books in order.

If you intend to someday borrow money from a bank or other financial institution, or a friend or loved one, having up-to-date and accurate financial records will go a long way in convincing them that you and your business are good investments. After all, your bookkeeping system is a reflection of you and your company. If your books are disorganized, then it can be assumed that the rest of your business is also in disarray. On the other hand, if your books are meticulously recorded and maintained — including all receipts, invoices, cancelled checks and bank statements — it suggests that other aspects of your business are in order.

CASH OR ACCRUAL

When it comes to accounting, there are two basic methods: cash or accrual. Each requires distinct types of record-keeping systems.

- **Cash basis of accounting**: With a cash-basis accounting system, a sale is made only when cash is received. Likewise, an expense is incurred only when you pay a bill (by cash, check or credit card.) Most small businesses use a cash basis for accounting because it's simpler than an accrual basis.

- **Accrual basis of accounting**: Given the realities of our credit-obsessed society, it's common for suppliers and vendors to grant or be granted credit, and for you to manage cash flow by delaying (within a specified time frame) payment to creditors. The accrual basis of accounting takes this reality into consideration.

With this system of accounting, each item or transaction is entered as earned or as an expense incurred regardless of when the actual payments are made or received. Sales that are made on credit are recorded at once in your books as sales and also in your accounts receivables (more about this type of account later). Expenses or disbursements that you incur on credit must similarly be recorded at the time they are incurred. Even if you have not paid them yet. These transactions will be recorded in your accounts payable account (more on this later) and your expense or disbursement account.

What is meant by an "Account?"

An account is the form of record used to list debits and credits in a single balance sheet category. Think of debits as monies coming into your business (pluses) and credits as monies going out of your business (minuses). Examples of the types of accounts your business is likely to use are: cash accounts (including checks) and credit cards, expense/disbursement accounts, accounts receivable and accounts payable.

Cash accounts include all cash, check or credit card transactions of money received by your business. Expense accounts also include cash, check and credit card accounts, but they reflect money going out, or that is disbursed. Accounts receivable are monies owed to you that have not yet been received, while accounts payable are monies that you owe venders or creditors that you haven't paid yet.

What is meant by a "Transaction?"

A transaction is an individual business activity, such as a tax payment you make or purchase order you process, as opposed to a series of activities in the same account, or category. Transactions are recorded in chronological/sequential order.

Journals and Ledgers

The transactions and accounts that you'll be tracking will be recorded in journals and ledgers, respectively. That is, transactions are recorded in journals, and accounts are recorded in ledgers.

Journals

The information about each business transaction is first recorded in a journal, a chronological (day-by-day) record of business transactions. Journal entries include the date of the transaction, the increase or decrease in the specific ledger account and a brief explanation of the transaction. At convenient intervals (say, once a day, or every other day) you'll want to transfer (post) these journal entries to their respective ledger accounts.

Your business journal for a mixed tape catalog company might look something like this:

Trans No.	Date	Description of Transaction	LP	Chk. No.	Receipt Amt. (Debit)	Disbursement Amount (Credit)	Balance
1.	3/25/07	Start-up capital (savings)		1005	$2,500		$2,500
2.	3/28/07	CD burning equipment		1006		$500	$2,000
3.	4/3/07	Blank cds (1,000)		1007		$300	$1,700
4.	4/14/07	Business cards (500)	1	Cash		$150	$1,550
5.	4/17/07	Flyers (500)		1008		$350	$1,200
6.							
7.							
8.							

Notice that the left side of the journal is called debit and the right side is called credit. In the field of accounting, accountants use *debit* to mean an entry on the left-hand side of an account and *credit* to mean an entry on the right-hand side.

Ledger

Instead of transactions, your ledgers will reflect activities in the various business accounts. Think of each account as a distinct *category* of business activities. Here's what your   might look like:

Date	Description of Activity	Receipt Amount (Debit)	Disbursement Amount (Credit)	Balance
4/12/07	Advance sale (re-order)	$100		$1,000
4/14/07	Purchased 500 bus. cards		$150	$850
4/16/07	Pre-order	$125		$975

Posting

The process of transferring the debits and credits from your general journal to the appropriate ledger accounts is called posting. Each amount listed in the debit column of the journal is *posted* by entering it on the debit side of an account in the ledger. Likewise, each amount listed in the credit column of the journal is posted to the credit side of a ledger account.

Step 1:   Locate in the ledger the first account name in the journal entry.

Step 2:   Enter into the debit column of the ledger account the amount of the debit as shown in the journal.

Step 3:   Enter the date of the transaction in the ledger account.

Step 4:   Enter in the reference column of the ledger account the number of the journal page from which the entry is being posted.

Step 5:   Return to the journal and enter in the LP (ledger page) column the number of the ledger account or page to which the debit was posted.

Step 6:   Now repeat the posting process described above for the credit side of the journal entry.

General Ledger

Trans. No.	Date	Description of Transaction	LP	Chk. No.	Receipt Amt. (Debit)	Disburse-ment Amt. (Credit)	Balance
1.	3/25/07	Start-up capital (savings)		1005	$2,500		$2,500
2.	3/28/07	CD burning equipment		1006		$500	$2,000
3.	4/3/07	Blank cds (1,000)		1007		$300	$1,700
4.	4/14/07	Business cards (500)	1	Cash		$150	$1,550
5.	4/17/07	Flyers (500)		1008		$350	$1,200
6.							
7.							
8.							

Cash Ledger

Date	Description of Activity	Receipt Amount (Debit)	Disbursement Amount (Credit)	Balance
4/12/07	Advance sale (pre-order)	$100		$1,000
4/14/07	Purchased 500 business cards		$150	$ 850
4/16/07	Pre-order	$125		$ 975

In actual practice, each account occupies its own page in a ledger.

Bookkeeping may seem tedious but it doesn't have to be. Once you get in the habit of doing it, it won't feel like drudgery. The greatest benefit of keeping up-to-date (advisably on a daily basis) and accurate records is that you'll be able to tell at a glance what's working and what's not. Plus, come tax time you won't have to panic because you either can't find certain records or they're all over the place.

chapter 16

TAXES GALORE

THERE'S NO GETTING AROUND it: if you plan to go into business — and stay in business — you're going to have to pay taxes! You might as well suck it up now. The good news, though, (just in case you need a little consolation), is that while tax evasion is against the law (26 USC 7201), tax *avoidance* isn't.

Quite simply, tax evasion occurs when a person or business entity fails to pay taxes they're required by law to pay, or when they reduce their tax liability by using illegal means. Tax avoidance is the minimization of tax liabilities by taking advantage of available tax deductions, tax credits and tax-deferral provisions of the Internal Revenue Code. More on this later.

Except for partnerships, which file *information returns*, all businesses are required to file an annual income tax return. Both types of returns serve the same purpose: to report your business's income, expenses, deductions and credits. (More on this later.) Whether your business makes money or loses money, you still have to file a tax return.

With over 500,000 pages of tax legislation currently on the books, this is not a subject you'd want to tackle on your own. Instead, make an investment in a good tax attorney that specializes in your type of business (for example, an entertainment law attorney or one who's an expert on import/export laws) and a certified public accountant. Don't be cheap; your investment in professional help will save you money in the long run. Even more, it can reduce the chances of your being audited. And, to top it off, you can deduct the expenses that come with hiring an attorney or Certified Public Accountant (CPA).

What Kinds of Taxes Will You Have To Pay?

There are literally dozens of different types of taxes, most of which are beyond the scope of this book. The primary ones that you should be concerned about are: income tax, sales tax, excise tax, self-employment tax, and employment taxes (if you have employees).

Income tax: A tax on the yearly profits from property, business pursuits, etc. Or, in the case of individual taxpayers, the tax on income, wages, salary, commissions, etc. You'll have to pay state *and* federal income tax.

Sales tax: Tax levied on the sale of goods based on their value.

Excise tax: This "miscellaneous" tax is imposed on the manufacture, sale, or consumption of commodities; upon licenses to pursue certain occupations (such as a liquor license or furnishing utility services) or upon corporate privileges (including the ability to sue in court). Examples include cigarettes and other tobacco products, petroleum products and highway use (for certain trucks, truck tractors and buses on public highways).

Self-employment tax: The tax collected for Social Security and Medicare contributions.

Employment taxes: This tax is required only if you have employees.

Social Security and Medicare taxes: *Your* share of Social Security and Medicare taxes *for your employees*. As a matter of law, you are required to withhold from employees' paychecks 7.65% for their contributions to Social Security and Medicare. Another 7.65% comes from your company's revenues, bringing the total contribution to 15.3%.

Federal unemployment taxes (FUTA): Together with state unemployment systems, federal unemployment taxes provide for payments of unemployment compensation to workers who have lost their jobs. Unlike Social Security and Medicare taxes, FUTA is not withheld from employees' wages. Your business pays this tax.

Below is a summary of the kinds of taxes you have to pay, depending on your business structure, and the IRS forms you'll be required to file. (See Appendix E for a more comprehensive list of tax forms.) Tax forms are available at many post offices and banks, and at local IRS offices.

Business Structure And Kind of Tax	Forms You'll Have to File
Sole Proprietorship	
Income tax	Form 1040 and Schedule C or C-EZ
Self-employment tax	1040 and Schedule SE
Estimated Tax	1040—ES
Excise taxes	
Employment taxes	Form 941
Social Security and Medicare Taxes and Income Tax Withholding	
Federal unemployment (FUTA) tax	Form 940 or 940-EZ
Depositing employment taxes	Form 8109
Partnership	
Annual return of income	Form 1065
Employment taxes	Same as sole proprietorship
Excise taxes	

(Individual Partner)

Income tax	Form 1040 and Schedule E
Self-employment tax	Form 1040 and Schedule SE
Estimated tax	Form 1040-ES

Corporation or S-Corporation

Income tax	Form 1120 or 1120-a (corporation)
	Form 1120s (S-corporation)
Estimated tax	Form 1120-w (corporation only) and Form 8109
Employment taxes	Same as sole proprietor
Excise taxes	

S-Corporation shareholder

Income tax	Form 1040 and Schedule E
Estimated tax	Form 1040-ES

If your business is a limited liability company (LLC), you will be required to inform the IRS which entity you want to be treated as for tax purposes — either a partnership or corporation — and file the appropriate forms.

When Do You Have to File Taxes?

Basically the IRS has a pay-as-you-go income tax system. That is, they require you to pay business income taxes around the same time that you're earning the income. That's what estimated taxes are all about. Rather than waiting until the end of the calendar or fiscal year to receive your tax payment, the IRS requires you to pay "estimated" taxes on a quarterly basis (every three months).

For business structures other than a corporation, you will have to pay estimated taxes on April 15, June 15, September 15 and January 15 of each year. This tax is due if you *expect* to owe taxes of $1,000 or more (after subtracting your withholding and credits) when you file your income tax return.

Corporate estimated taxes are due on the 15th day of the fourth, sixth, ninth and twelfth month after the end of the company's *fiscal* year, which may not necessarily be the same as the January-to-December calendar year. A fiscal year can be any consecutive twelve-month period.

Corporate estimated taxes are due if you expect to owe $500 or more (in income tax less credits) when you file your tax return. Meanwhile, corporate federal tax returns are due on the 15th day of the third month after the end of the company's fiscal year. So, for example, if your company's fiscal year is April — March, you'd be required to file corporate federal tax returns by June 15.

If you weren't convinced in Chapter 15, "Keeping Track of Your Money," about the need to maintain accurate and up-to-date records you should be at this point. Even if you hire a tax attorney or CPA (and you should) to do the grunt work of properly organizing and preparing your records and tax forms, it's important that you keep your records in order. This will make it easier on them, and probably cost you less since attorneys and accountants usually charge by the hour.

How Much In Taxes Do You Have To Pay?

Depending on the business structure you choose, tax rates can be as high as 39.6% for sole proprietorships, the same as for individual taxpayers, or as low (well, maybe not low, but you know what I mean) as 15% for C-Corporations.

Here's a breakdown of federal income tax rates for unmarried individuals (other than surviving spouses and heads of households) and corporations, as of November 17, 2006.

Unmarried Individuals:
(Other than Surviving Spouses and Heads of Households)

If taxable income is:	The tax is:
Not over $22,100	15% of the taxable income
Over $22,100 but not over $53,500	$3,315 plus 28% of the excess over $22,100
Over $53,500 but not over $115,000	$12,107 plus 31% of the excess over $53,500
Over $115,000 but not over $250,000	$31,172 plus 36% of the excess over $115,000
Over $250,000	$79,772 plus 39.6% of the excess over $250,000

Corporations

If taxable income is:	The tax is:
$1 - $50,000	15%
$50,001 - $75,000	25%
$75,001 - $10,000,000	34%

If over $100,000, tax is increased by
the lesser of:
1. 5% of excess or
2. $11,750

$10,000,000+	35%

If over $15,000,000 tax is increased by
the lesser of:
1. 3% of excess or
2. $100,000

Government As Your Business Partner

Notwithstanding all the taxes that are heaped on business owners (and everyone else, for that matter), the government has an incentive to work *with* you. When you're a business owner, the law is on your side — unless you break the law or fail to pay taxes. Then…well, you know the rest.

Simply put, without taxes the federal (and state) government would not be able to operate. It would not be able to provide such services as police, fire, and public schools. So what does the government do? It allows business owners all manner of tax deductions (or write-offs) and credits to lessen (that's right, lessen) their tax burden.

Specifically, the federal government is aware that the more employees who are on your payroll the more taxes it will likely collect. As such, the government makes tax credits available to companies that hire *qualified* employees. It's quid pro quo, something for something.

Tax Credits are subtracted *directly* from the amount of taxes that would otherwise be owed, instead of being subtracted from income before taxes are computed. ***Tax Deductions*** allow taxpayers to deduct specified percentages from amounts spent on business expenses. They come in two general categories:

- Standard deductions (governed by 26 USC 144 [a])
- Itemized deductions (governed by 26 USC 161-188), which are expenses that are allowed as deductions from your gross income, itemized in detail under appropriate headings, and subtracted to arrive at your taxable income.

Another way that the government will work with you as a business owner is by allowing you to pay taxes *after* you've paid business expenses and taken advantage of allowable tax deductions and credits. This is significant because individual taxpayers pay the government taxes *before* they even get to take care of their own living expenses.

Here's what the difference looks like:

Individual	**Business**
Taxable Income (gross pay)	Income (gross revenue)
⇩	⇩
Taxes	Business Expenses
	(deductions and credits)
⇩	⇩
Living Expenses (net pay)	"Taxable" Income
	⇩
	Taxes
	⇩
	Net (business) Income

As you can see, the order in which you pay taxes significantly affects how much of *your* money you'll ultimately end up keeping. By exhausting business expenses, deductions and credits *before* paying taxes you in effect lower your taxable income and, quite possibly, your tax rate.

Section 26 U.S.C. 162 [a] of the tax code allows you to deduct business-related expenses that are "ordinary" and "necessary" for the operation of your business. This language is decidedly broad, leaving a lot of room for interpretation. In short, it means that expenses should be normal and common for the type of business you own, or the industry that your business is in. Expenses should also be helpful (that is, they should either increase revenues or reduce expenses) and proper.

Appendix F contains a list of some of the kinds of business tax deductions you might be able to take advantage of. The list is not comprehensive. Your tax attorney should be able to help you identify and maximize appropriate tax deductions. If you can't afford to retain a tax attorney, your best bet is to seek free advice from a Service Corps of Retired Executives (SCORE) counselor or Small Business Development Centers (SBDC) volunteer familiar with business tax law.

chapter 17

MANAGING RISK

THE MOMENT YOU DECIDED to put on your entrepreneurial cap you became a risk taker. There's the risk that your business may fail; the risk that you'll lose friends and become estranged from relatives; that you'll lose personal savings or other assets in the process of starting up or running your business; that your investment of time and energy may not pay off the way you'd planned, and so on, and so on.

My point is that when it comes to business, risk is unavoidable. The key is to plan ahead, and calculate your risks. Even more important, you need to *manage* risk. Getting insurance coverage is the ideal way to manage risk.

No question, insurance is one of those vexing aspects of business that you would rather do without. Like taxes. In fact, dishing out hard-earned cash for insurance premiums can feel like a tax. Insurance is one of those things that you don't think you need — until you *really* need it. But by then you will have lost, perhaps indefinitely, whatever it was that you should've protected (with insurance coverage) in the first place.

In order to manage any kind of business-related risk you must first understand exactly what risks you're likely to encounter. A simple way to do this is to take out a blank piece of paper and list all possible risks that could affect your business. From there you can begin designing an insurance program that specifically fits your business's needs and risks. For example, you wouldn't want to pay for hurricane insurance if you live in New York City, any more than you'd think it prudent to get vandalism and malicious mischief coverage if your business is home-based. Pay for exactly what you think you'll need, and avoid duplicative insurance.

One final note on developing an insurance program: Since the needs and risks of your business will change from time to time, you will want to review your program periodically.

Types of Coverage

Basic fire insurance: Covers damage done to your business as a result of a fire.

Business interruption insurance: In case of power failure, a fire, storm, hurricane or other unforeseen peril, this type of coverage will come in handy.

Crime or theft insurance: If your business is located in a high-risk area where robberies, burglaries and employee theft are common, make it your business to get federal crime insurance.

Disability insurance: Covers employees for loss of income should they become disabled *off* the job. You can also cover yourself for loss of income if you are disabled.

Health insurance: Covers medical, dental, vision and other coverage intended to maintain and promote employee health and wellness. Healthcare costs can be expensive.

Key-man insurance: Protects your business against financial loss due to the death of a partner or invaluable employee.

Liability insurance: Covers your legal liabilities stemming from accidents and injuries.

Life Insurance: Pays whomever you designate as a beneficiary a lump sum of money if you die. This type of insurance is usually affordable.

Partnership or corporation insurance: This type of coverage enables surviving partners or shareholders to retire (or sell) their interests upon their partner's or fellow shareholder's death.

Product liability insurance: If *anyone* could hurt themselves by using your products, it would be a smart move to get this type of insurance.

Property or "all-risk" coverage: In addition to coverage for fire damage, this extended, all-encompassing coverage insures your business against possible loss of property due to smoke, earthquake, storms, explosions and other disasters.

Sole proprietorship insurance: This is a form of business life insurance. It provides for maintenance of your business if you were to die.

Unemployment insurance: This kind of insurance is required by federal and state law if you have one or more employees who work for you at least 20 weeks in a calendar year. It provides a fixed income to employees who lose their job through no fault of their own.

Vandalism and malicious mischief coverage: Covers against property losses caused by vandalism and similar activities.

Vehicle insurance: Protects against theft and collision, cost of repairs, injuries and accidents with uninsured drivers.

Workers' compensation: This is disability and death benefits to employees (or their beneficiaries, in the case of death) hurt on the job. It covers medical expenses and loss of income. In some states, like New York, workers' compensation is mandated if you have even one employee.

chapter 18

GIVE AND TAKE

A S A BUSINESS OWNER, you'll no doubt have to do some negotiating to realize your goals. Said another way, negotiating is an integral part of business.

Contrary to what is often portrayed in movies and on TV, the objective of negotiating is not about coming out on top, getting your way or being right. It's not a zero-sum game where one party wins and the other necessarily loses. That's not negotiating. That's competing.

As the title of this chapter suggests, negotiations are about give and take. They're about making concessions and bargaining, so that in the end you *and* the other party win. Keep in mind that the other party is not your enemy.

If you view the other party as a partner you'll be less likely to try to exploit the situation. Plus, you never know: you may want to do business with them in the future. Chances are if they feel manipulated or disrespected during the negotiation process, they won't want to do business with you again. Even worse, they may spread the word about your abrasive, predatory tactics.

The terms and conditions of most contracts can be negotiated. Don't assume that because a certain contract is simple or "standard" that you can't negotiate to add, modify or delete specific clauses. You can. This goes for bank loan and car loan contracts, and vendor/supplier contracts, too. You don't have to settle for terms and conditions you don't agree with. While negotiations don't always result in an agreement, they should never conclude with either party feeling ill will. The way to go about the negotiation process is to set goals and limits *before* the actual negotiations begin. You need to be clear-headed, not too emotional. Know in advance what you want to take away from the negotiations, and what you're willing to give up, or concede, in return. Of course, you should never reveal all your cards before or during negotiations.

And remember, this is not all about you. While organizing your thoughts and making preparations for the eventual negotiations, consider what's important to the other party. What might they want? What might their boundaries be?

When negotiation time comes, don't be so eager to get the process over with. Do more listening than talking. You'll learn a lot by letting the other party reveal their position first. Let them name a price. If they're hesitant to make the first offer, present an initial offer on the extreme high side. Of course you don't really expect them to accept the offer. What you're doing is putting a feeler out, trying to get a sense of the ballpark area that the other party is comfortable with. Once you've got them talking, responding with counter offers, you will be able to go back and forth with each other until a win-win situation is reached. Bear in mind that sometimes no agreement is reachable. Either you or the other party may decide that a contractual agreement would not be in your best interest. Should you run into this situation remain respectful, and, when appropriate, ask the other party to refer you to someone who might be a better fit for what you're trying to accomplish.

chapter 19

DOTTING "I'S" AND CROSSING "T'S"

B ACK IN THE DAY, a verbal agreement and a handshake would adequately seal a deal. But they won't cut it in the fast-paced, litigious world we live in. To be on the safe side, commit all business agreements to writing. And whatever you do, read the contract thoroughly before signing it.

Overly eager to secure a particular deal, or not wanting to come across as unknowledgeable or indecisive, many entrepreneurs rush to sign contracts that they really don't understand; contracts that are based on little more than good faith. This is a big mistake. A signature on a contract implies that the signatory, or person who signed it, read, understood and agreed to the terms and conditions contained in it.

Unless a contract is very basic, you should hire a small business lawyer who specializes in the type of contract you might be asked to sign, one who has years of experience and who understands the decidedly confusing legal jargon. Again, you might want to seek assistance from a SCORE counselor who has a legal background, or contact your local or regional bar association for guidance.

CONTRACT BASICS

A contract is a legally enforceable promise or set of promises. It obligates two or more parties to carry out a specific deed, or to not do

181

something that is within their legal authority. What gives contracts a notable character is the assurance that you can rely on the courts to make sure that they are honored. That is, you can sue the other party or parties for breach of contract. Just remember that it can go the other way, too: you can be sued if you fail to carry out or honor a contract.

Contracts are either bilateral or unilateral. In bilateral contracts, both parties make a promise or promises. Only one party makes a promise or promises in a unilateral contract. Additionally, contracts may be deemed valid, voidable or void.

Valid contracts meet all of the legal requirements for a binding contract and are enforceable in court. Conversely, an unenforceable contract is one that meets the basic legal requirement for a contract but may not be enforceable due to some other legal rule, such as a statute of limitation.

Voidable contracts are those in which one or more of the parties have the legal right to cancel their promise or obligations under the contract. This might occur when fraud or duress is involved. A *void* contract is not actionable at all. By this I mean neither party is obligated to honor this kind of agreement. Also, there is no legal redress; you can't sue for breach of contract. An example of a void contract is a "contract" to kill someone.

5 FUNDAMENTAL ELEMENTS OF A CONTRACT

1. *Mutual Agreement*: After negotiations, this is the first step toward bringing about a contract. Basically an offer is made, and an offer is accepted. The party making the offer (offeror) must presently intend to enter into the contract upon acceptance of specific terms. He or she must communicate his or her offer (preferably in writing) to the party being asked to accept the offer (the offeree).

   Similarly, the offeree must have a present intent to accept the offer. He or she must likewise communicate his or her acceptance of the other party's terms.

2. *Voluntarily made*: Parties must go into contracts willingly. They must consent. The use of force, coercion, fraud, unfair persuasion or trickery will make a contract voidable.

3. *Capacity to contract*: This means the *ability* to take on legal obligations and acquire legal rights. Usually capacity to contract is presumed once a person reaches the legal age of maturity, all else being equal. Minors, persons suffering from mental illnesses or defects, and intoxicated persons are considered to lack capacity to go into a contractual agreement.

4. *Legal objectives*: Obviously the motive behind a contract should be to make a legal agreement.

5. *Consideration*: No, I'm not talking about being courteous. Consideration is anything of legal value that is bargained for and given in exchange for an act or promise. Consideration doesn't have to be in the form of money.

Here's a sample book publishing contract, used with permission, from *Business and Legal Forms for Authors and Publishers* (3rd edition) by Tad Crawford.

Book Publishing Contract

AGREEMENT, entered into as of this _____ day of _____, 20___, between _____ (hereinafter referred to as the "Publisher"), located at _____, and _____ (hereinafter referred to as the "Author"), located at _____.

WHEREAS, the Author wishes to create a book on the subject of _____ (hereinafter referred to as the "Work")

WHEREAS, the Publisher is familiar with the work of the Author and wishes to publish a book by the Author; and

WHEREAS, the parties wish to have said publication performed subject to the mutual obligations, covenants, and conditions herein.

NOW, THEREFORE, in consideration of the foregoing premises and the mutual covenants hereinafter set forth and other valuable considerations, the parties hereto agree as follows:

1. **Grant of Rights.** The Author grants, conveys, and transfers to the Publisher in that unpublished Work titled _____, certain limited, exclusive rights as follows:

   (A) To publish, distribute, and sell the Work in the form of a _____ book;

   (B) In the territory of _____;

   (C) In the_____ language; and **(D)** For a term of _____years.

2. **Reservation of Rights.** All rights not specifically granted to the Publisher are reserved to the Author, including but not limited to electronic rights which are defined as rights in the digitized form of works that can be encoded, stored, and retrieved from such media as computer disks, CD-ROM, computer databases, and network servers.

3. **Delivery of Manuscript.** On or before the _____ day of _____, 20_____, the Author shall deliver to the Publisher a complete manuscript of approximately _____ words, which shall be reasonably satisfactory in form and content to the Publisher and in conformity with any outline or description attached hereto and made part hereof. The manuscript shall be in the following form: ❏ double-spaced hard copy ❏ computer files (specify format _____). The manuscript shall include the additional materials listed in Paragraph 4 (except that if an index is to be provided by the Author, it shall be delivered to the Publisher within thirty days of Author's receipt of paginated galleys). If the Author fails to deliver the complete manuscript within ninety days after receiving notice from the Publisher of failure to deliver on time, the Publisher shall have the right to terminate this Agreement and receive back from the Author all monies advanced to the Author pursuant to Paragraphs 4, 5, and 9. If the Author delivers a manuscript which, after being given detailed instructions for revisions by the Publisher and _____ days to complete such revisions, is not reasonably acceptable to the Publisher, then monies advanced to the Author pursuant to Paragraphs 4, 5, and 9 shall be ❏ retained by the Author ❏ repaid to the Publisher ❏ repaid to the Publisher only in the event the Author subsequently signs a contract with another Publisher for the Work.

4. **Additional Materials.** The following materials shall be provided by the Author _____ _____. The cost of providing these additional materials shall be borne by the Author, provided, however, that the Publisher at the time of signing this Agreement shall give a nonrefundable payment of $_____ to assist the Author in defraying these costs, which payment shall not be deemed an advance to the Author and shall not be recouped as such.

5. **Permissions.** The Author agrees to obtain all permissions that are necessary for the use of materials copyrighted by others. The cost of providing these permissions shall be borne by the Author, provided, however, that the Publisher at the time of signing this Agreement shall give a nonrefundable payment of $_____ to assist the Author in defraying these costs, which payment shall not be deemed an advance to the Author and shall not be recouped as such. Permissions shall be obtained in writing and copies shall be provided to the Publisher when the manuscript is delivered.

6. Duty to Publish. The Publisher shall publish the Work within _____ months of the delivery of the complete manuscript. Failure to so publish shall give the Author the right to terminate this Agreement ninety days after giving written notice to the Publisher of the failure to make timely publication. In the event of such termination, the Author shall have no obligation to return monies received pursuant to Paragraphs 4, 5, and 9.

7. Royalties. The Publisher shall pay the Author the following royalties: ____ percent of the suggested retail price on the first 5,000 copies sold; ____ percent of the suggested retail price on the next 5,000 copies sold; and ____ percent of the suggested retail price on all copies sold thereafter. These royalty rates shall be discounted only in the following circumstances: _____

_____

All copies sold shall be cumulated for purposes of escalations in the royalty rates, including revised editions, except for editions in a different form (such as a paperback reprint of a hardcover original) which shall be cumulated separately. Copies sold shall be reduced by copies returned in the same royalty category in which the copies were originally reported as sold.

In the event the Publisher has the right pursuant to Paragraph 1(A) to publish the Work in more than one form, the royalty rates specified above shall apply to publication in the form of a _____ book and the royalty rates for other forms shall be specified here: _____

_____

_____

8. Subsidiary Rights. The following subsidiary rights may be licensed by the party indicated and the proceeds divided as specified herein:

Subsidiary Right	Right to License		Division of Proceeds	
	Author	Publisher	Author	Publisher
_____	_____	_____	_____	_____
_____	_____	_____	_____	_____
_____	_____	_____	_____	_____
_____	_____	_____	_____	_____
_____	_____	_____	_____	_____

If the division of proceeds for any subsidiary right changes after the sale of a certain number of copies, indicate which right, the number of copies required to be sold, and the new division of proceeds _____

_____

_____

The Publisher shall have no rights pursuant to this Paragraph 8 if Publisher is in default of any of its obligations under this Agreement. The right to license any subsidiary right not set forth in this Paragraph is retained by the Author. Licensing income shall be divided as specified herein without any reductions for expenses.

Licensing income shall be collected by the party authorized to license the right and the appropriate percentage remitted by that party to the other party within ten days of receipt. Copies of all licenses shall be provided to both parties immediately upon receipt.

9. Advances. The Publisher shall, at the time of signing this Agreement, pay the Author a nonrefundable advance of $_____, which advance shall be recouped by the Publisher from payments due to the Author pursuant to Paragraph 11 of this Agreement.

10. Accountings. Commencing as of the date of publication, the Publisher shall report every ____ months to the Author, showing for that period and cumulatively to date the number of copies printed and bound, the number of copies sold and returned for each royalty rate, the number of copies distributed free for publicity purposes, the number of copies remaindered, destroyed, or lost, the royalties paid to and owed to the Author, and licensing income. If the Publisher sets up a reserve against returns of books, the reserve may only be set up for the four accounting periods following the first publication of the Work and shall in no event exceed 15 percent of royalties due to the Author in any period.

11. Payments. The Publisher shall pay the Author all monies due Author pursuant to Paragraph 10 within thirty days of the close of each accounting period.

12. Right of Inspection. The Author shall, upon the giving of written notice, have the right to inspect the Publisher's books of account to verify the accountings. If errors in any such accounting are found to be to the Author's disadvantage and represent more than 5 percent of the payment to the Author pursuant to the said accounting, the cost of inspection shall be paid by the Publisher.

13. Copyright and Authorship Credit. The Publisher shall, as an express condition of receiving the grant of rights specified in Paragraph 1, take the necessary steps to register the copyright on behalf of the Author and in the Author's name and shall place copyright notice in the Author's name on all copies of the Work. The Author shall receive authorship credit as follows: _____.

14. Warranty and Indemnity. The Author warrants and represents that he or she is the sole creator of the Work and owns all rights granted under this Agreement, that the Work is an original creation and has not previously been published (except for those materials for which permissions have been obtained pursuant to Paragraph 5), that the Work does not infringe any other person's copyrights or rights of literary property, nor, to his or her knowledge, does it violate the rights of privacy of, or libel, other persons. The Author agrees to indemnify the Publisher against any final judgment for damages (after all appeals have been exhausted) in any lawsuit based on an actual breach of the foregoing warranties. In addition, the Author shall pay the Publisher's reasonable costs and attorney's fees incurred in defending such a lawsuit, unless the Author chooses to retain his or her own attorney to defend such lawsuit. The Author makes no warranties and shall have no obligation to indemnify the Publisher with respect to materials inserted in the Work at the Publisher's request. Notwithstanding any of the foregoing, in no event shall the Author's liability under this Paragraph exceed $_____ or _____ percent of sums payable to the Author under this Agreement, whichever is the lesser. In the event a lawsuit is brought which may result in the Author having breached his or her warranties under this Paragraph, the Publisher shall have the right to withhold and place in an escrow account _____ percent of sums payable to the Author pursuant to Paragraph 11, but in no event may said withholding exceed the damages alleged in the complaint.

15. Artistic Control. The Author and Publisher shall consult with one another with respect to the title of the Work, the price of the Work, the method and means of advertising and selling the Work, the number and destination of free copies, the number of copies to be printed, the method of printing and other publishing processes, the exact date of publication, the form, style, size, type, paper to be used, and like details, how long the plates or film shall be preserved and when they shall be destroyed, and when new printings of the Work shall be made. In the event of disagreement after consultation, the Publisher shall have final power of decision over all the foregoing matters except the following, which shall be controlled by the Author_____ _____. No changes shall be made in the complete manuscript of the Work by persons other than the Author, except for reasonable copy editing, unless the Author consents to such changes. Publisher shall provide the Author with galleys and proofs which the Author shall review and return to the Publisher within thirty (30) days of receipt. If the cost of the Author's alterations (other than for typesetting errors or unavoidable updating) exceeds _____ percent of the cost of the typography, the Publisher shall have the right to deduct such excess from royalties due Author hereunder.

16. Original Materials. Within thirty days after publication, the Publisher shall return the original manuscript and all additional materials to the Author. The Publisher shall provide the Author with a copy of the page proofs, if the Author requests them prior to the date of publication.

17. Free Copies.

18. Revisions. The Author agrees to revise the Work on request by the Publisher. If the Author cannot revise the Work or refuses to do so absent good cause, the Publisher shall have the right to have the Work revised by a person competent to do so and shall charge the costs of said revision against payments due the Author under Paragraph 11 for such revised edition. In no event shall such revision costs exceed $ _____ .

19. Successors and Assigns. This Agreement may not be assigned by either party without the written consent of the other party hereto. The Author, however, shall retain the right to assign payments due hereunder without obtaining the Publisher's consent. This Agreement shall be binding on the parties and their respective heirs, administrators, successors, and assigns.

20. Infringement. In the event of an infringement of the rights granted under this Agreement to the Publisher, the Publisher and the Author shall have the right to sue jointly for the infringement and, after deducting the expenses of bringing suit, to share equally in any recovery. If either party chooses not to join in the suit, the other party may proceed and, after deducting all the expenses of bringing the suit, any recovery shall be shared equally between the parties.

21. Termination. The Author shall have the right to terminate this Agreement by written notice if: **(A)** the Work goes out-of-print and the Publisher, within ninety days of receiving notice from the Author that the Work is out-of-print, does not place the Work in print again. A work shall be deemed out-of-print if the work is not available for sale in reasonable quantities in normal trade channels; **(B)** if the Publisher fails to provide statements of account pursuant to Paragraph 10; **(C)** if the Publisher fails to make payments pursuant to Paragraphs 4, 5, 9, or 11; or **(D)** if the Publisher fails to publish in a timely manner pursuant to Paragraph 6. The Publisher shall have the right to terminate this Agreement as provided in Paragraph 3. This Agreement shall automatically terminate in the event of the Publisher's insolvency, bankruptcy, or assignment of assets for the benefit of creditors. In the event of termination of the Agreement, the Publisher shall grant, convey, and transfer all rights in the Work back to the Author.

22. Production Materials and Unbound Copies. Upon any termination, the Author may, within sixty days of notification of such termination, purchase the plates, offset negatives, or computer drive tapes (if any) at their scrap value and any remaining copies at the lesser of cost or remainder value.

23. Promotion. The Author consents to the use of his or her name, portrait, or picture for promotion and advertising of the Work, provided such use is dignified and consistent with the Author's reputation.

24. Arbitration. All disputes arising under this Agreement shall be submitted to binding arbitration before _____ in the following location _____ and shall be settled in accordance with the rules of the American Arbitration Association. Judgment upon the arbitration award may be entered in any court having jurisdiction thereof.

25. Notice. Where written notice is required hereunder, it may be given by use of first class mail addressed to the Author or Publisher at the addresses given at the beginning of this Agreement and shall be deemed received five days after mailing. Said addresses for notice may be changed by giving written notice of any new address to the other party.

26. Entire Agreement and Modifications. This Agreement represents the entire Agreement between the parties. All modifications of this Agreement must be in writing and signed by both parties.

27. Waivers and Defaults. Any waiver of a breach or default hereunder shall not be deemed a waiver of a subsequent breach or default of either the same provision or any other provision of this Agreement.

28. Governing Law. This Agreement shall be governed by the laws of _____ State.

IN WITNESS WHEREOF, the parties have signed this Agreement as of the date first set forth above.

Author_____   Publisher_____
                                                                             Company Name

                                                  By_____
                                                                  Authorized Signatory, Title

Breach of Contract

For any number of reasons, a party to a contract may fail, without legal excuse, to perform a promise that forms the whole or part of a contract. In other words, he may breach the contract. If this happens (assuming you're not the party who breached the contract), you may have several legal remedies at your disposal.

Small Claims Court: This is a special court that provides speedy, informal and inexpensive legal redress of small claims. Parties normally represent themselves in these proceedings, and the amount in dispute is usually under $5,000.

State Court of Claims: These courts are more formal, and proceedings can take months or even years to adjudicate a claim. Unlike in small claims court, there is no statutory monetary cap on the amount that can be sued for.

Arbitration: There may be times when you'll want to hold another party accountable for a breach of contract but won't want to seek redress through the courts. In this case, arbitration might be an appealing alternative. Rather than having a judge weigh the merits of each party's case before rendering a decision, in arbitration an impartial third person is *chosen by the parties* to resolve the dispute. Both parties must agree in advance to abide by the arbitrator's decision.

chapter 20

INTELLECTUAL PROPERTY

KEEPING IT OFFICIAL, WHEN it comes to business, imitation is not the highest form of flattery. In fact, it usually means theft, infringement and knockoffs, all of which translate to a loss of customers, market share, reputation and revenues. So be careful who you share your business ideas and trade secrets with. By trade secret I mean the private knowledge (i.e., information, design, process, technique or formula) that gives you, the owner, a competitive business advantage. Think Kentucky Fried Chicken or Coca Cola. Even though this private knowledge is not tangible property like a piece of machinery, it's still your property. So if it's necessary to share a trade secret with, say, potential investors or employees, first have them sign "keep-confidential agreements."

In the chapter 17, *"Managing Risk,"* you learned why it's important to devise an insurance program to protect your business's tangible property. In this chapter you'll find out how to protect your intangible, or intellectual, property.

What Exactly Is Intellectual Property?

An idea, invention, unique name, expression, business method, chemical formula or industrial process are all examples of intellectual property. What they have in common is that they're derived from the human mind or intellect.

Obviously you cannot touch, hear, smell, taste or see an *idea*. This is because ideas are intangible. What makes something like an expression or business method intellectual *property* is that it has some value in the marketplace (that is, people will pay for it or, in the case of a business process, it can generate revenue) and can ultimately be reduced to a tangible form. And as with protecting the tangibles of your business, you should plan ahead when it comes to safeguarding your creations.

The three basic forms of protection for intellectual property are patents, trademarks and copyrights. Each offers legal protection (sometimes referred to as "offensive rights") for different kinds of creations. And each type of right is transferable by sale or gift, or by will or inheritance.

As far as patents and trademarks go, it is common for individuals or companies to license their ownership rights. In this way, the inventor of a patent or creator of a trademark avoids having to spend what can amount to huge sums of money to manufacture goods, market services or implement business processes. Instead they license *their* intellectual property on agreed-upon terms and conditions in exchange for royalties, or a percentage of sales. Licensing by itself can be very lucrative.

Patents

A patent provides legal protection for inventions. It gives you, the patent owner, the right to prohibit others from making, using or selling your mental concept or creation for up to twenty years from the date you file your application with the Patent and Trademark Office (PTO). Protection, however, extends only throughout the U.S., its territories and possessions. It will not protect you outside the U.S.

There are three different types of patents:

Utility Patents cover inventions that function in a unique manner. They are utilitarian in nature. *Design patents*, by far the most common type of patent applied for, cover the unique, aesthetic or visible shape or design of an invention. Finally, *plant patents* cover asexually reproducible plants, through the use of cuttings and grafts.

Getting a patent is much more difficult than, say, getting a copyrighted work registered. It's advisable to hire a registered patent attorney or agent to help you with this complicated process.

For starters, your invention must be deemed by the patent examiner to be a novelty. That is, it must be different from what is already known to the public. There cannot be identical or indistinguishably similar inventions. Any earlier patents relating to your invention are known as "prior art."

In addition to being new, your invention must be nonobvious *at the time you came up with it.* With so many patent applications being received daily by the PTO, this second test can be a hard one to satisfy. By nonobvious, the PTO means that your invention must be adequately different from what has already been invented or described before, to a person with ordinary skill in the area of technology related to your invention. For example, if you tried to patent a board game strikingly similar to Monopoly® (except yours would be based on your neighborhood), chances are the PTO would deny your application. The likely reason: the concept is not sufficiently different from Monopoly®. It is fairly obvious, or foreseeable.

You may want to make certain "claims" to an invention *before* actually filing an application for a patent. This can be accomplished by filling out and submitting to the PTO what is called a provisional patent application. (Provisional applications apply only to utility patents.) This will block or bar someone else from making identical claims in a subsequent patent application. There's a filing fee of $75.

Within one year of filing the provisional application you must file a regular patent application. In the interim, your application will be considered "patent pending." This status does not fully prevent others from filing for a regular patent after the one-year expiration of the provisional application. It merely puts the PTO on notice of your intentions to file a regular patent application.

For small (business or personal) entities, the utility patent application filing fee is $345, the design patent application fee is $155, and the plant application fee is $240. These fees don't include the exorbitant hourly fees for patent searches, agents or attorneys. They also do not include the separate and distinct *issue fees* and *maintenance* fees.

Issue fees: If the patent examiner at the PTO decides to accept your *utility* patent application, you'll then be required to pay a utility patent application issue fee of $605. You will be given three months to pay this fee. A design patent application issue fee will set you back $215, and a plant patent application issue fee costs $290.

Maintenance fees: These fees only apply to utility patents and must be paid to keep the patent in effect for the entire 20-year term. There's a six-month window in which to pay each fee. Payment of the three maintenance fees are as follows:

Maintenance fee I, payable 3-3 ½ years after issuance ($415)
Maintenance fee II, payable 7-7 ½ years after issuance ($950)
Maintenance fee III, payable 11-11 ½ years after issuance ($1,455)

You can get a patent application, fee schedule and other related information from the (PTO):

Patent and Trademark Office
2900 Crystal Drive
Arlington, VA 22202
(703) 305-8600
www.uspto.gov

Trademarks

When most people think of trademarks the first thing that usually comes to mind is a logo. Indeed, logos can be trademarked but so can designs, sounds, shapes, smells and even colors.

A trademark basically is your company's brand name. It's the "symbol" that comes to mind when people think of your business.

It's any word or symbol that you consistently use in marketing goods and/or services that identifies and distinguishes your company from others in the marketplace.

You don't want prospective customers to confuse your business with another's, or vice versa. Either scenario could cost your business revenue. By registering your trademark with the Patent and Trademark Office your business will be given a monopoly over the use of the symbol registered. Unlike patents and copyrights, there is no statutory term limit on trademarks.

Trademark rights can be kept as long as the trademark continues to be used. That is, as long as it is attached to, or forms part of, a product. The trademark symbol is "TM," or ® for "registered."

The filing fee for registering a trademark is $325. Along with the fee you must include: a completed application form, a drawing of the trademark and three samples showing the actual use of your mark. For example, if your mark will be used on stationery and business products, include sample sketches of these applications. Mind you, if you think that you'll only need to protect the integrity of your symbol within the geographical boundaries of your state, then you can simply have it trademarked on the state level. The fees will vary from state to state, but they will be a lot cheaper than a federal trademark, probably in the area of $50 to $120. But if you want nationwide protection the only way to go about it is through the PTO.

If instead of selling products your business offers services, you wouldn't want a "trade" mark. Rather, you'd want to get a service mark. The fees are the same as for registering a trademark.

Copyrights

A copyright grants authors, artists, composers and the like the right to prevent others from copying or commercially using their original expressions without permission. It also gives the copyright owner the right to recover damages from those who infringe on their right.

You cannot copyright an idea! Copyright only protects the concrete *expression* of an idea.

The moment you write or otherwise create a work (such as a book or musical recording) it is considered automatically copyrighted. It's just not *registered*. So if someone came along and registered *your* "original" work before you did, they'd be deemed the owner of the work. If a work was created under a "work-made-for-hire contract," the employee or independent contractor creates the work *for* an employer — not herself. In this case, the employer owns the copyright to the work.

As some form of protection, you should place the copyright notice (copyright © 2006 Jane Doe) on those works that you desire copyright coverage on. Again, it's not the same as actually registering the copyrighted work, but it at least lets others know who the real creator of the work is.

Getting an original work registered is easy. All you have to do is fill out a copyright application with the copyright office (which is part of the Library of Congress in Washington, DC) and send the completed application to them with the required $30 fee. Also, send them two examples of the work you want registered.

The address is:

Copyright Office
Library of Congress
101 Independence Ave. S.E.
Washington, DC 20231
(202) 707-9100
www.loc.gov

The term of copyright coverage is the life of the creator of the work plus 70 years. For works made-for-hire and for anonymous and pseudonymous work, the term is a flat 95 years from publication or 120 years from creation, whichever is shorter.

Chapter 21

MAKE IT HAPPEN

FOR ME, BOTH MY business and life goals revolve around teaching. At the core of my being, I am an educator. In one way or another, I've been a teacher since fourth grade, although I couldn't name it or claim it as a gift back then. In those days, what I knew was that I loved books and I loved to learn. I loved books so much, in fact, that I was willing to make forays into enemy territory to get them; the only library in my neighborhood was near housing projects whose residents had an ongoing war with the people in my projects. And I knew, too, that I wanted my siblings to enjoy the indescribable pleasures that come from learning. Whenever I had to baby-sit them, rather than spend whole days watching TV, we'd spend part of the day playing school. I was their teacher, of course. And they were my eager students. Over time, I became aware of my talent for teaching.

Unfortunately, it took my coming to prison to learn that just being aware of my talents and gifts was not enough. That was only half the equation. There are countless gifted and amazingly talented men and women serving lengthy sentences behind prison walls. In fact, talent comes a dime a dozen. All of us, if we'd only look deep enough, will discover our gifts and talents.

The other half of the equation required me to apply my gifts, consistently apply them and stay the course, all of which I learned to do behind prison walls. It was while teaching my first class on personal finance to fellow prisoners in June 1995 that I finally embraced my personal power. I realized how much joy I got from teaching, and how engaged and interested people were in what I had to say. I felt a sense of power, a sense of purpose. That was my "Aha" moment. I knew then that I was meant to teach.

Since then, I have been teaching as many incarcerated men as possible about the worlds of business and investing, exposing them to a different way of looking at themselves and money. Different ways that can help them lead law-abiding and productive lives once they eventually return to society.

I have learned that through teaching and counseling I am best able to relate to others, to connect with them in a meaningful way. Through teaching and counseling, my natural capacity to empathize with others and my ability to feel and express compassion flourish. In helping others identify and tap into their talents and good qualities—their personal power—I am able to see reflections of my own personal power. I become more focused on my goals in life, on the legacy I want to leave behind.

The book you are now reading is part of my legacy. And to write it, I had to take the advice I've given you: I had to plan my work and work my plan.

I'll admit, after I got over the intoxicating excitement of starting a book for the incarcerated and formerly incarcerated—a business book at that—I began to have doubts as to whether I could actually complete it. Initially, I was intimidated by the amount of time, commitment and research writing this type of book would demand of me. I'm sure some of my uncertainty came from the fact that over the years I'd begun, but never finished, several books. But I was determined to see this book to fruition. I was determined to make it happen!

The first thing I did was take out a few sheets of paper and begin brainstorming about the kinds of topics and information I thought would motivate my intended audience (you) to really think *outside* the cell. I wanted to make sure the book had all the pertinent business and legal information to get you started on your way to realizing your dreams.

After hours of excited brainstorming, and a few days of trying to make sense of the multi-directional scribbling I'd put down on paper, my initial book outline began to take shape. I went back and forth with various chapter titles until I felt I had ones that captured the essence of what I wanted to say. I placed topics and information from my brainstorming session in bullet format underneath appropriate chapter headings.

There was no way I could predict how the final book would turn out. All I knew was that I'd give it my best. I was very fortunate to have a professional writer as my wife. I sent her a copy of my initial chapter outline, and she helped me rearrange and organize my thoughts. She helped to make sure that I had a smooth, logical flow in the way the chapters unfolded.

I knew from the beginning that if I wanted to complete this project, if I wanted to overcome bouts of self-doubt, I had to break this project down to size. I had to make it manageable, doable.

At the time, I was a facilitator for the prison's Transitional Services Program, where I conducted daily orientation classes for men who were new to the facility. My program assignment consumed six hours of my day, affording me little time to dedicate to writing a book.

As much as I enjoyed teaching, I decided to change my program to something that did not require as much of my time. I changed to a pantry job in the mornings and evenings. Basically, I served breakfast and dinner chow to the men in my housing unit for all of 20 minutes. I had the rest of the day to do as I pleased. Well, not exactly, but you know what I mean.

With my edited outline as my guide, I carved out three hours every morning (my thinking is clearest in the morning). Instead of setting out to write a book, I focused on writing four to six pages a day. Often I wrote more. Pages turned into chapters, and chapters turned into the *completed* book you are now reading.

It took me three months to write the first draft of this book, and another six or seven months of revising and editing. Actually, my wife (and later, her sister) did the bulk of the editing. I did cursory edits while writing the pages and chapters, but I didn't want to get lost in the editing process, as many people do. I simply wanted to write. I wanted to unleash my thoughts, not curtail them. So I just let the words flow from me to the paper. Five edits later, I had my completed manuscript.

Whatever you set your mind to, you can accomplish. It all starts with having the right attitude, the right mindset.

Let me tell you, though, simply having a bunch of ideas won't cut it. I can't count the number of times people approach me with one business idea or another; they fantasize about the millions of dollars their businesses will earn, the mansions they'll own, the luxury cars they'll collect, etc., etc. When I ask them to show me their *written* plan—not the ideas swirling around in their heads—they draw a blank.

"I don't have a written plan…but I'm telling you, my business will be successful," they say. "I've got it all mapped out. I just need to get out of prison. I'm telling you…"

I smile knowingly. I've heard this line time and again.

"I don't doubt you," I tell them, "but you have to write your ideas down on paper; think them through, organize them and map them out strategically. You can't keep it all in your head. Right now all you have is a bunch of ideas. Everyone's got ideas. And most of them go nowhere. Do you know why?"

"Because they don't write them down?" they respond teasingly.

"That's right. When you write your plans down they become real. It's like writing a contract with yourself. It's a commitment to yourself. Plus, rather than trying to remember all the different aspects of your plans, you'll have a tangible document to refer to any time you need to."

Their nods tell me that they get my point. Not that they'll actually write their plans down. Most do not. It's too daunting for them; it's much easier to simply keep ideas swirling in their heads, easier to simply talk about what they intend to do and have.

The sad truth is that many people live in a fantasy world, a world of wishful thinking. I hope you're not one of them. Whether your goal is to operate a mom-and-pop store or build a business empire, you will have to put in the hard work necessary to realize your dreams. You will have to sacrifice time and energy to make it happen. There are no short cuts, no easy roads to success.

Your business plans must be based in reality! You must be willing to fully commit yourself to your dreams; you must be willing to plan your work and work your plan. As long as you consistently put one foot in front of the other, you *will* achieve your business and life goals.

* * *

This may sound like a cliché, but writing this book has truly been a labor of love. It's one of my proudest accomplishments. It would not have been possible if I'd only fantasized about writing a book. This book would not have materialized if I hadn't made certain changes in how I managed my time. It would not have become a reality if I hadn't shared my vision with my wife, and a select few other supportive people, who encouraged me throughout to put one foot in front of the other, to keep my eyes on the prize, to make it happen.

* * *

This book is your ultimate blueprint for success. But you must take the first step. *You* have to make it happen! You are *not* your mistakes! You are not your past. Excuses, no matter how you dress them up, no matter how you rationalize them, just won't cut it. Plain and simple, you can't "come up" if you're too busy staying down. It's impossible. And it goes against everything this book is about.

My long-term vision is that *Think Outside the Cell* will not only become a mindset that empowers men, women and young adults warehoused in prisons across the country, as well as those who were formerly incarcerated, but that it will flourish into a dynamic and influential movement. A movement based on personal development and responsibility, healthy families, and community and economic empowerment.

I hope this book has been as motivating to read as it has been for me to write.

Now make it happen!

Appendix A

Business Resources

U. S. Small Business Administration
409 Third Street, SW
Washington, DC 20416
(800) U-ASK-SBA
www.sba.gov
A government agency created to support and promote entrepreneurs. The SBA offers free and inexpensive pamphlets on a variety of business subjects.

Service Corps of Retired Executives Association (SCORE)
409 Third Street, SW, 6th Fl.
Washington, DC 20024
(800) 634-0245
www.score.org
SCORE is the premier source of free and confidential small business advice for entrepreneurs. SCORE has over 10,500 volunteers at 389 chapter offices nationwide.

U.S. Small Business Administration
Office of Small Business Development Centers
409 Third Street, SW
Washington, DC 20416
(800) U-ASK-SBA
www.sba.gov/sbdc

SBDCs offer one-stop assistance to individuals and small businesses by providing a wide variety of information and guidance in easily accessible branch locations. The program is a cooperative effort of the private sector, the educational community and federal, state and local governments.

National Association of Women Business Owners
8405 Greensboro Drive, Suite #800
McLean, VA 22102
(800) 55-NAWBO
www.national@nawbo.org
The voice of America's 10.4 million women-owned businesses.

Entrepreneurs Only
(formerly Young Entrepreneurs Organization, "YEO")
500 Montgomery Street, Suite 500
Alexandria, VA 22314
(703) 519-6700
www.eonetwork.org
Global community of business owners—all of whom run companies that earn more than $1 million—that encourages direct peer-to-peer learning.

Junior Achievement (JA)
One Education Way
Colorado Springs, CO 80906
(719) 540-8000 or (800) 843-6395
www.ja.org

Using hands-on experiences, JA brings the real world to students in grades K-12 to help young people understand the economies of life.

Ewing Marion Kauffman Foundation
4801 Rockhill Road
Kansas City, MO 64110
(816) 932-1000
www.kauffman.org
The only large American foundation to focus on entrepreneurship. The Kauffman Foundation focuses its grant-making and operations on advancing entrepreneurship and improving the education of children and youth.

U.S. Small Business Administration
Small Business Investment Companies (SBIC)
409 Third Street, SW
Washington, DC 20416
www.sbaonline.sba.gov
SBICs are privately organized and managed venture capital firms licensed by the U.S. Small Business Administration to make equity capital or long-term loans available to small companies.

Accion International
56 Roland Street, Suite 300
Boston, MA 02129
(617) 625-7080
www.accion.org
International organization that gives people the tools they need to work their way out of poverty, by providing micro loans and business training to poor women and men who start their own businesses.

U.S. Chamber of Commerce
1615 H Street, NW
Washington, DC 20062-2000

(202) 659-6000 or (800) 638-6582

www.uschamber.com

The world's largest business federation, representing more than 3 million businesses of all sizes, sectors and regions before Congress, the White House, regulatory agencies, the courts and governments around the world.

National Association for the Self-Employed (NASE)

P.O. Box 612067

DFW Airport

Dallas, TX 75261-2067

(800) 232-6273

www.nase.org

NASE is the nation's leading source for the self-employed and businesses with up to ten employees.

Direct Marketing Association (DMA)

1120 Avenue of the Americas

New York, NY 10036-6700

(212) 768-7277

www.the-dma.org

The leading global trade association of business and nonprofit organizations using and supporting direct marketing tools and techniques.

Direct Selling Association (DSA)

1667 K Street, NW

Suite 1100

Washington, DC 20006-1660

(202) 452-8866

www.dsa.org

The DSA is the national trade association of the leading businesses that manufacture and distribute goods and services sold directly to consumers.

American Small Business Association
206 E. College Street
Suite 201
Grapevine, TX 76051
(800) 942-2722
www.asbaonline.org
A partnership of individuals and business owners with the shared goal of prosperity and realization of the American Dream.

The National Foundation for Women Business Owners (NFWBO)
1100 Wayne Avenue
Suite 830
Silver Spring, MD 20910
(301) 608-2590
www.nfwbo.org
A lobbying organization (with a nonprofit research foundation) aimed at promoting policies that encourage entrepreneurship by women.

National Business Incubation Association (NBIA)
20 E. Circle Drive
Suite 37198
Athens, OH 45701-3571
(740) 593-4331
www.nbia.org
NBIA is the world's leading organization advancing business incubation and entrepreneurship. It is composed primarily of incubator developers and managers.

U.S. Department of Commerce
Minority Business Development Agency
1401 Constitution Avenue, NW
Washington, DC 20230
(888) 342-1551

www.mbda.gov

The only federal agency created specifically to foster the establishment and growth of minority-owned businesses in the U.S.

International Franchise Association (IFA)
1501 K Street, NW
Suite 350
Washington, DC 20005
(202) 628-8000
www.franchise.org
The IFA protects, enhances and promotes franchising.

National Federation of Independent Business (NFIB)
53 Century Blvd.
Suite 250
Nashville, TN 37214
(800) NFIB-NOW
www.nfib.org

NFIB is the largest advocacy organization representing small and independent business in Washington, D.C., and all 50 state capitals.

Appendix B

Recommended Reading

GENERAL BUSINESS

Rich Dad Poor Dad by Robert T. Kiyosaki with Sharon L. Lechter (Scottsdale. AR: Tech Press, Inc., 1997)

Rich Dad's Retire Young Retire Rich by Robert T. Kiyosaki with Sharon L. Lechter (New York, NY: Warner Business Books, 2002)

Entrepreneurship: Starting and Operating a Small Business by Steve Mariotti (Upper Saddle River, NJ: Prentice Hall, 2007)

Negotiate Your Way to Riches: How to Convince Others to Give You What You Want by Peter Wink (Franklin Lake, NJ: Career Press, 2003)

Think and Grow Rich: A Black Choice by Dennis Kimbro (New York: Fawcett Columbine, 1991)

Think and Grow Rich by Napoleon Hill (Napoleon Hill Foundation, 2005)

Start Your Own Business: The Only Start-Up Book You'll Ever Need by Rieva Lesonski & Entrepreneur Magazine Staff (Irvine, CA: Entrepreneur Magazine Press, 2004)

Make it Happen: A Hip Hop Generation Guide to Success by Kevin Liles (New York, NY: Simon & Schuster, 2005)

Enterprising Women: Lessons from 100 of the Greatest Entrepreneurs of Our

Day by A. David Silver (Saranac Lake, NY: AMACOM, 1994)

INC. Yourself: How To Profit By Setting Up Your Own Corporation, 10th ed. by Judith . McQuown (Franklin, PA: Career Press, INC., 2004)

*The Power of Positive Thin*king, miniature edition, by Norman Vincent Peale (Philadelphia, PA: Running Press Books, 2002)

The Martha Rule by Martha Stewart (Gordonville, VA: Rodale Press, 2005)

Young Entrepreneur's Guide to Business Terms by Steplan Schiffman (Watts Reference Series, 2003)

Russell Simmons' Laws of Success by Russell Simmons with Chris Morrow (New York, NY: Gotham Books, 2007)

Good to Great: Why Some Companies Make the Leap…and Others Don't by Jim Collins (New York: Harper Collins, 2001)

BIOGRAPHIES

Why Should White Guys Have All the Fun by Reginald F. Lewis and Blair S. Walker (Hoboken, NJ: Wiley 2005)

About My Sister's Business: The Black Woman's Road Map to Successful Entrepreneurship by Fran Harris (New York, NY: Simon & Schuster, 1996)

Succeeding Against All Odds by John H. Johnson and Lerone Bennett (New York, NY: Amistad Press, Import of Harper Trade, 1993)

Black Titan: A. G. Gatson and the Making of a Black American Millionaire by Carol Jenkins (New York, NY: One World/Ballentine, 2003)

Direct from Dell: Strategies That Revolutionized an Industry by Michael Dell and Catherine Fredman (Collingdale, PA: Diane Pub. Co., 1999)

Sam Walton: Made in America by Sam Walton (Doubleday, Canada, Ltd., 2003)

Life & Death: Sex, Drugs, Money & God by Russell Simmons & Nelson George (New York, NY: Three River Press: Crown Pub. Group, 2002)

Entrepreneurs in Profile by Steve Mariotti, with Tony Towle, et. al. (Franklin Lakes, NJ: Career Press, 2000)

How to Succeed in Business Without Being White by Earl G. Graves (New York, NY: Harper Business, 1998)

MANAGEMENT

Winning by Jack Welch & Suzy Welch (New York, NY: Harper Business, 2005)

The 7 Habits of Highly Effective People by Stephen Covey (New York, NY: The Free Press, 2004)

How to Become a Great Boss: The Rules for Getting and Keeping the Best Employees by Jeffrey J. Fox (New York, NY: Hyperion Press, 2002)

Managing for the Future by Peter F. Drucker (New York, NY: Penguin Group, 1993)

Managing for Dummies by Peter Economy and Bob Nelson (IDG Books Worldwide, INC., 2003)

The Effective Executive by Peter F. Drucker (New York, NY: Harper Information, 2005)

Who Moved My Cheese? by Spencer Johnson (New York, NY: Penguin Group, 1998)

Managing for the First Time by Cherry Mill (Wappingers Fall, NY: Beekman Books, 2000)

Excellence in Nonprofit Leadership by Peter F. Drucker, et. al. (Hoboken, NJ: Wiley, 1998)

MARKETING / SALES

5 Steps to Successful Selling by Zig Ziglar (Upper Saddle River, NJ: Prentice Hall, 1996)

The 22 Immutable Laws of Marketing by Al Ries and Jack Trout (New York, NY: Harper Business, 1999)

Swim With the Sharks Without Being Eaten Alive by Harvey B. Mackay and Kenneth H. Blanchard (New York, NY: Harperbusiness, 2005)

Ziglar on Selling by Zig Ziglar (Nashville, TN: Thomas Nelson, 2003)

Power Netweaving: 10 Secrets to Successful Relationship Marketing by Robert S. Littell & Donna Fisher (National Underwriter Co., 2001)

The Sales Bible by Jeffrey H. Gitomer (New York, NY: Wiley, 2003)

Guerrilla Marketing: Secrets for Making Big Profit from Your Small Business, 3rd rev. ed. by Jay Conrad Levinson (Boston, MA: Houghton Mifflin Co., 1998)

Little Red Book of Selling: The 12.5 Principles of Sales Greatness: How To Make Sales Forever by Jeffrey H. Gitomer (Austin, TX: Bard Press, 2004)

The Greatest Salesman in the World by George Og Mandino (New York, NY: Bantam Books, 1999)

Buzz Marketing: Get People to Talk About Your Stuff by Mark Hughes (New York, NY: Portfolio Hardcover, 2005)

Steal These Ideas by Steve Cone (New York, NY: Bloomberg Press, 2005)

FINANCE/ACCOUNTING

Accounting for Dummies, 3rd ed. by John A. Tracy (New York, NY: Wiley, 2004)

Accounting the Easy Way, 4th ed. by Peter J. Eisen (Hauppauge, NY: Barron's Educational Series, 2003)

The Complete Idiot's Guide to Accounting by Lita Epstein and Shellie C. Moore (New York, NY: Penguin Group Inc., 2003)

Financing Your Business Dreams With Other People's Money by Harold R. Lacy (Traverse City, MI: Rhodes and Easton, 1998)

TAXES

Doing Business Tax Free: Perfectly Legal Techniques for Reducing or Eliminating Your Federal Business Taxes by Robert Cooke (Hoboken, NJ: Wiley, 2001)

Finance and Tax Planning for the Home-Based Business by Charles Lickson & Bryane Lickson (Menlo Park, CA: Crisp Pub. Co., 1996)

Taxes for Dummies by Eric Tyson (Hoboken, NJ: Wiley, 1996)

BUSINESS PLAN WRITING

How to Write a Business Plan, 7th ed. by Mike McKeever (Berkeley, CA: Nolo Press, 2005)

Business Plans for Dummies by Paul Tiffany and Steven D. Peterson (Hoboken, NJ: Wiley, 2004)

Rich Dad's Advisors: The ABC's of Writing Winning Business Plans: How to Prepare a Business Plan That Others Will Want to Read by Garrett Sutton (New York, NY: Warner Books, 2005)

Business Plans That Work: A Guide for Small Business by Jeffrey A. Timmons, Andrew Zacharakis and Stephen Spinelli (New York, NY: McGraw-Hill Education, 2004)

Entrepreneur's Complete Sourcebook by Alexander W. Hiam (Upper Saddle River, NJ: Prentice Hall, 1996)

Mancuso's Small Business Resource Guide, Revised and Updated by Joseph Mancuso (Naperville, IL: Sourcebooks, 1996)

MAGAZINES

You can get the following magazines and other publications at a discount from:

Delta Publishing Group, Ltd.
1243 48th Street
Brooklyn, NY 11219
www.deltamagazines.com

Entrepreneur
Black Enterprise
Hispanic Business
INC
BusinessWeek: Small Biz

WEB SITES

www.nfte.com
www.pepweb.org
www.myownbizkit.com
www.ja.org
http://acenet.csusb.edu
www.irs.gov
www.raisecapital.com
www.eonetwork.org

Legislative Committees on Small Business

U. S. Senate

Small Business Committee
Washington, DC 20510
www.Senate.gov

U.S. House of Representatives

Small Business Committee
Washington, DC 20515
www.house.gov/smbiz

State Legislative Committees

Alabama

Alabama Senate
Business and Labor Committee
Alabama State House
11 South Union Street
Montgomery, AL 36130

Alabama House of Representatives
Subcommittee on Business & Labor
Alabama State House

11 South Union Street
Montgomery, AL 36130

Alaska
Alaska Senate
Senate Labor & Commerce Committee
State Capitol
Juneau, AK 99801-1182

Alaska House of Representatives
House Labor & Commerce Committee
State Capitol
Juneau, AK 99801-1182

Arizona
Arizona State Senate
Commerce & Economic Development Committee
Capitol Complex
1700 West Washington
Phoenix, AZ 85007-2890

Arizona House of Representatives
Commerce Committee
Capitol Complex
1700 West Washington
Phoenix, AZ 85007-2890

Arkansas
Arkansas Senate
Insurance & Commerce Committee
State Capitol, Rm 320
Little Rock, AR 72201

Arkansas House of Representatives
Insurance & Commerce Committee

State Capitol, Rm 350
Little Rock, AR 72201

California
California State Senate
Business, Professions & Economic Development Committee
State Capitol
P.O. Box 942849
Sacramento, CA 95814

California State Assembly
Committee on Business & Professions
State Capitol
P.O. Box 942849
Sacramento, CA 95814

Colorado
Colorado State Senate
Business, Labor & Technology Committee
Colorado State Capitol
200 East Colfax
Denver, CO 80203

Colorado House of Representatives
Business Affairs & Labor Committee
Colorado State Capitol
200 East Colfax
Denver, CO 80203

Connecticut
Connecticut State Senate
Senate Commerce Committee
Capitol Building, Rm 110
Hartford, CT 06106

Connecticut House of Representatives
Commerce Committee
Capitol Building, Rm 110
Hartford, CT 06106

Delaware
Senate Small Business Committee
Legislative Hall
P.O. Box 1401
Dover, DE 19903

House Business/Corporations/Commerce Committee
Legislative Hall
P.O. Box 1401
Dover, DE 19903

Florida
Senate Committee on Commerce & Consumer Services
404 South Monroe Street
Tallahassee, FL 32399-1100

House Business Regulation Committee
300 House Office Building
402 South Monroe Street
Tallahassee, FL 32399-1300

Georgia
Senate Economic Development & Tourism Committee
State Capitol 321-B Coverdell Off. Bldg.
Atlanta, GA 30334

Georgia General Assembly Economic Development
& Tourism Committee
State Capitol, Rm 228
Atlanta, GA 30334

Hawaii
Senate Business & Economic Development Committee
Hawaii State Capitol
415 South Beretania Street
Honolulu, HI 96813

House Economic Development
& Business Concerns Committee
Hawaii State Capitol
415 South Beretania Street
Honolulu, HI 96813

Idaho
Senate Commerce & Human Resource Committee
State Capitol Building
P.O. Box 83720
Boise, Idaho

House Commerce & Human Resource Committee
State Capitol Building
P.O. Box 83720
Boise, Idaho

Illinois
Senate Commerce & Economic Development Committee
Capitol Building
Springfield, IL 62706

House International Trade & Commerce Committee
Capitol Building
Springfield, IL 62706

Indiana
Senate Commerce, Economic Development

& Small Business Committee
200 W. Washington Street
Indianapolis, IN 46204-2785

House Agriculture & Small Business Committee
200 W. Washington Street
Indianapolis, IN 46204

Iowa
Senate Business & Labor Relations Committee
State Capitol
Des Moines, IA 50319

House Commerce, Regulation & Labor Committee
State Capitol
Des Moines, IA 50319

Kansas
Senate Commerce Committee
State Capitol
300 SW 10th Street
Topeka, KS 66612

House Commerce & Labor Committee
State Capitol
300 SW 10th Street
Topeka, KS 66612

Kentucky
Senate Licensing, Occupations
& Administrative Regulation Committee
State Capitol Annex
Frankfort, KY 40601

House Agriculture & Small Business Committee
State Capitol Annex
Frankfort, KY 40601

Louisiana
Senate Commerce Committee
State Capitol
900 North 3rd Street
Baton Rouge, LA 70802

House Commerce, Consumer Protection & International Affairs
State Capitol
900 North 3rd Street
Baton Rouge, LA 70802

Maine
Senate Business, Research
& Economic Development Committee
State Capitol
1 State House Station
Augusta, ME 04333

House Business, Research
& Economic Development Committee
State Capitol
1 State House Station
Augusta, ME 04333

Maryland
Senate Education, Business & Administration Subcommittee
State House
100 State Circle
Annapolis, MD 21401

House Business Regulation Subcommittee
State House
100 State Circle
Annapolis, MD 21401

Massachusetts
Senate Community Development
& Small Business Joint Committee
State House, Rm 39
Boston, MA 02133

House Community Development
& Small Business Joint Committee
State House
Boston, MA 02133

Michigan
Senate Economic Development,
Small Business & Regulator Reform
P.O. Box 30036
Lansing, MI 48909-7536

House Commerce Committee
P.O. Box 30014
Lansing, MI 48909-7514

Minnesota
Senate Commerce Committee
Capitol Building
75 Rev. Martin Luther King. Jr. Blvd.
St. Paul, MN 55155-1606

House Commerce & Financial Institutions Committee
100 Rev. Dr. Martin Luther King Jr. Blvd.
St. Paul, MN 55155

Mississippi
Senate Business & Financial Institutions Committee
State Capitol
501 N. West Street
Jackson, MS 39201

House Banking and Financial Services Committee
State Capitol
501 N. West Street
Jackson, MS 39201

Missouri
Senate Small Business, Insurance
& Industrial Relations Committee
State Capitol Building
201 West Capitol Avenue
Jefferson City, MO 65101

House Small Business Committee
State Capitol Building
201 West Capitol Avenue
Jefferson City, MO 65101

Montana
Senate Business, Labor & Economic Affairs Committee
State Capitol
1301 East Sixth Avenue
Helena, MT 59620

House Business & Labor Committee
State Capitol
1301 East Sixth Avenue
Helena, MT 59620

Nebraska
Unicameral Legislative Committee on Business & Labor
State Capitol
P.O. Box 94604
Lincoln, NE 68509-4604

Nevada
Senate Commerce & Labor Committee
State Capitol
101 North Carson Street
Carson City, NV 89701

Assembly Commerce & Labor Committee
State Capitol
101 North Carson Street
Carson City, NV 89701

New Hampshire
Senate Energy & Economic Development Committee
State House
107 North Main Street
Concord, NH 03301

House Commerce Committee
State House, Rm 302
107 North Main Street
Concord, NH 03301

New Jersey
Senate Commerce Committee
State House
Trenton, NJ 08625

Assembly Commerce & Economic Development Committee
State House
Trenton, NJ 08625

New Mexico
Senate Corporations & Transportation Committee
State Capitol
Santa Fe, NM 87501

House Business & Industry Committee
State Capitol
Santa Fe, NM 87501

New York
Senate Commerce, Economic Development
& Small Business Committee
State Capitol
Albany, NY 12247

Assembly Small Business Committee
State Capitol
Albany, NY 12247

North Carolina
Senate Commerce Committee
State Capitol
One East Endenton Street
Raleigh, NC 27699

House Commerce Committee
State Capitol
One East Endenton Street
Raleigh, NC 27699

North Dakota
Senate Industry, Business & Labor Committee
State Capitol
600 East Boulevard
Bismark, ND 58505-0360

House Industry, Business & Labor Committee
State Capitol
600 East Boulevard
Bismark, ND 58505-0360

Ohio
Senate Insurance, Commerce & Labor Committee
State Capitol
77 South High Street
Columbus, OH 43215

House Commerce & Labor Committee
State Capitol
77 South High Street
Columbus, OH 43215

Oklahoma
Senate Business & Labor Committee
State Capitol
2300 N. Lincoln Boulevard
Oklahoma City, OK 73105

House Business & Economic Development Committee
State Capitol
2300 N. Lincoln Boulevard
Oklahoma City, OK 73105

Oregon
Senate Economic Development Agency Oversight Committee
State Capitol
900 Court Street
Salem, OR 97301-4047

House Business, Labor & Consumer Affairs Committee
State Capitol
900 Court Street
Salem, OR 97301-4047

Pennsylvania
Senate Community Economic Development Committee
State Capitol Building
Harrisburg, PA 17120

House Commerce Committee
State Capitol Building
Harrisburg, PA 17120

Rhode Island
Senate Commerce, Housing
& Municipal Government Committee
State House
Providence, RI 02902

House Corporation Committee
State House
Providence, RI 02902

South Carolina
Senate Labor, Commerce & Industry Committee
State Capitol Complex
P.O. Box 142
Columbia, SC 29202-0142

House Labor, Commerce & Industry Committee
State Capitol Complex
P.O. Box 11867
Columbia, SC 29211-1867

South Dakota
Senate Commerce Committee
State Capitol Building
Pierre, SD 57501-5070

House Commerce Committee
State Capitol Building
Pierre, SD 57501-5070

Tennessee
Senate Commerce, Labor & Agriculture Committee
State Capitol
Nashville, TN 37243

House Commerce Committee
State Capitol
Nashville, TN 37243

Texas
Texas Senate
Senate Business & Commerce Committee
P.O. Box 12068
Capitol Station
Austin, TX 78711

Texas House of Representatives
House Business & Industry Committee
P.O. Box 2910
Austin, TX 78768-2910

Utah
Utah State Senate
Senate Business & Labor Committee
W115 Capitol Complex
Salt Lake City, UT 84114

Utah House of Representatives
House Business & Labor Committee
W030 Capitol Complex
Salt Lake City, UT 84114

Vermont
Senate Committee on Economic Development,
Housing & General Affairs
Vermont State House
115 State Street
Montpelier, VT 05633-5301

House Committee on Commerce
Vermont State House
115 State Street
Montpelier, VT 05633-5301

Virginia
Virginia Senate
Senate Commerce & Labor Committee
P.O. Box 396
Richmond, VA 23218

Virginia House of Delegates
Commerce & Labor Committee
General Assembly Building
P.O. Box 406
Richmond, VA 23218

Washington
Senate Labor, Commerce, Research & Development Committee
229 Modular Building 2
P.O. Box 40466
Olympia, WA 98504-0466

House Commerce & Labor Committee
John L. O'Brien Bldg., 2nd Fl.
P.O. Box 40600
Olympia, WA 98504-0600

West Virginia
Senate Economic Development Committee
State Capitol Complex
Charleston, WV 25305

House of Delegates Industry & Labor
Economic Development & Small Business Committee
State Capitol Complex
Charleston, WV 25305

Wisconsin
Senate Committee on Veterans,
Homeland Security & Military Affairs,
Small Business & Government Reform
State Capitol
Madison, WI 53708

Assembly Committee on Small Business
State Capitol
Madison, WI 53708

Wyoming
Senate Minerals, Business
& Economic Development Committee
State Capitol Building
Cheyenne, WY 82002

House Minerals, Business
& Economic Development Committee
State Capitol Building
Cheyenne, WY 82002

Appendix D

New York State Occupational Licensing Survey

Prepared by

225 Varick St.
New York, NY 10014
tel: (212) 243-1313
fax: (212) 675-0286
email: lacinfo@lac.org
www.lac.org

Introduction

Over one hundred occupations in New York State require some type of license, registration, or certification by a state agency. This survey provides information about statutory restrictions placed on licensure of individuals with criminal records and about the procedures available to appeal a denial of licensure, registration, or certification based on an individual's criminal history.

For over thirty years, the Legal Action Center has worked with individuals with criminal records who are seeking employment. Our experience is that many people, including individuals with criminal records and those who counsel them, mistakenly believe that persons with criminal records are barred from obtaining most occupational licenses. As a result, many individuals with criminal records do not pursue employment opportunities that otherwise might have been available to them.

This survey can assist individuals with criminal records, employment counselors, and others who work with them to identify those State licenses for which they are eligible. (This survey does not cover federal licenses or other federal employment barriers.) The survey shows that there are only a few statutes that automatically bar individuals with criminal records from licensure solely on the basis of past convictions, and most of those statutes provide for lifting the automatic bar when an individual is granted a Certificate of Relief from Disabilities, a Certificate of Good Conduct, or Executive Clemency (pardon).

Although Certificates of Relief and Good Conduct lift automatic bars, individuals with criminal records may still be denied licenses based upon their conviction records. Licensing agencies are required by Article 23-A of the New York Correction Law (§§ 750-55) to make licensing decisions on a case-by-case basis. The law prohibits an agency from denying an individual with a criminal record a license because of his or her conviction record unless the individual's conviction(s) is (are) "directly related" to the specific license sought or the issuance of the license would create "an unreasonable risk to property or to the safety" of people (§ 752).

In determining job-relatedness and risk to the public or to property, licensing agencies must consider the following factors:

1. New York's public policy to encourage the licensing and employment of individuals with criminal records;

2. The specific duties and responsibilities necessarily related to the license being applied for, and the bearing, if any, that the individual's criminal history will have on his or her fitness to perform these duties and responsibilities;

3. The time that has elapsed since the individual's criminal conduct, and the individual's age at the time of the occurrence;

4.   The seriousness of the individual's offense(s);

5.   The legitimate interest of the licensing agency in protecting property, specific persons, or the general public; and

6.   Any evidence of rehabilitation that an individual with a criminal record presents, including a Certificate of Relief from Disabilities or Certificate of Good Conduct. (Certificates of Relief and Good Conduct create a presumption of rehabilitation.)

In determining whether a particular individual's convictions are, or are not, so related to the licensure sought as to justify a denial, licensing agencies must proceed on a case-by-case basis.

Some other statutes do not contain any automatic bar for individuals with criminal records but do restrict licensure or certification to persons of "good moral character." The meaning of this requirement may vary depending upon the licensing agency and the occupation or profession involved; more often than not, however, an applicant's criminal history *will* be taken into account as reflecting on his or her moral character. Again, the criminal record should be evaluated in accordance with Article 23-A.

How to Use This Survey

The first column of the survey lists occupations in alphabetical order. The occupational titles are taken from the statutory language, and thus may not necessarily be the most common title. For example, "Doctor" is listed as "Physician," and "Lawyer" as "Attorney."

The second column, "Agency," provides the name of the city or state agency that issues that particular license. A list of addresses and phone numbers for the agencies is attached as Appendix B.

The third column lists any information found in the licensing statute concerning specific restrictions placed on individuals with criminal records. The column specifies whether the restriction is mandatory (meaning that the licensing agency *may not* issue a license to someone with this conviction), or discretionary. For example, an applicant for licensure as an Alcoholic Beverage Manufacturer is automatically barred if s/he has been convicted of a felony or of certain offenses listed in the statute. On the other hand, an applicant for licensure as a barber or wrestler *may* be denied a license because of a conviction or because of having consorted with someone with a conviction. In some instances, the statute differentiates between people applying for licenses versus those who are convicted of a crime after holding a license.

The information about criminal record restrictions is followed by a citation to the statute containing the restriction. If the statute imposes a different restriction for people who are applying for the license, as opposed to those who are convicted of crimes once they hold a license, then the column explains that distinction as well.

The fourth column describes the circumstances under which a bar may (or in some cases, must) be lifted, such as after passage of a certain amount of time, at the discretion of the licensing agency, or upon receipt of a pardon.

The fifth column, "Related Restrictions or Requirements," lists information about restrictions or requirements that may not bar an individual with a criminal record from licensure but are likely to have some bearing on whether the licensure or certification will be issued. The most common example is a "Good Moral Character" requirement. For example, applicants for licenses issued by the State Education Department, which is responsible for issuing licenses for such medical occupations as nursing, opthalmic dispensing, and occupational therapy and certifications for, among others, the fields of psychology, teaching, social work, and shorthand reporting, must show good moral character.

The fifth column also states whether the applicant for licensure must be fingerprinted or bonded. Fingerprints are usually used to request a copy of the applicant's Criminal History Record from the State Division of Criminal Justice Services (DCJS). If the applicant is required to be bonded, the bonding agency will probably inquire into criminal records and have access to the DCJS file. Thus, even though there may be no specific criminal record restrictions listed for a particular license, other requirements or restrictions may affect an individual with a criminal record's application for licensure.

If an applicant is denied a license based on a criminal record, s/he may appeal the decision in one of several ways. Some licensing statutes have specific provisions for hearings, written appeals or court proceedings that an applicant may pursue. Those provisions are listed in the fifth column, "Appeal Procedures." Many licensing statutes do not specifically provide for appeals. "N/A" indicates that no statute directly specifies procedures for appealing the denial of that particular license. This does not mean, however, that the applicant is without recourse. An arbitrary denial of licensure based on criminal history may usually be challenged in a court proceeding brought under Article 78 of the Civil Practice Law and Rules (CPLR). This type of proceeding usually requires the assistance of legal counsel.

For further information about a particular license, consult the issuing agency.

The study does *not* include a complete survey of State and City Civil Service positions or of municipal licenses. Nor does it include criminal record bars imposed in certain industries, such as the home health care or trucking industries. These bars may apply even to individuals with a license to work in that industry.

About the Legal Action Center

The Legal Action Center is a non-profit, public interest organization whose primary purpose is to combat discrimination based on a person's criminal record, history of drug or alcohol abuse, or HIV status. The Center does this by educating individuals, their counselors, and employers that such discrimination is illegal and by providing legal representation as well as policy advocacy.

For individuals with criminal records living in New York State, the Center provides advice about their rights and assists them to develop job-seeking strategies, helps them "clean up" their criminal records and obtain Certificates of Relief and Good Conduct, and provides legal representation to challenge illegal denial or termination of employment and licensure. The Center has helped many individuals obtain licenses as taxi drivers, social workers, nurses, doctors, insurance agents, locksmiths and teachers. The Center's staff also helps those who have suffered discrimination in areas such as medical care, housing, insurance, and access to government benefits.

The Center also provides services to organizations that work with individuals with criminal records, drug and alcohol problems and HIV/AIDS, including training, technical assistance, and representation on issues relating to discrimination and to the confidentiality of alcohol and drug abuse treatment records and HIV-related information.

The Center has a variety of publications for both counselors and clients about the rights of individuals with criminal records, drug and alcohol problems, and HIV/AIDS. The Center also plays a leading role in addressing public policy issues that are important to these communities.

The survey initially was conducted with funding from the New York State Department of Probation and Correctional Alternatives and was revised with funding from the New York State Division of Criminal Justice Services.

OCCUPATION	AGENCY	CRIMINAL RECORD RESTRICTIONS	REMOVAL OF CRIMINAL RECORD RESTRICTIONS	RELATED RESTRICTIONS	RIGHTS AND APPEAL PROCEDURES
1. Accountant	State Ed Dept	None		Good moral character, ADBD -CPA: Educ L 7404(1)(7) -Public: Educ L 7405(3) *Any information about criminal record referred to OPD for investigation and determination.	Hearing Written appeal 8 NYCRR 28
2. Acupuncturist	State Ed Dept	None		Good moral character, ADBD Educ L §6506 *Any information about criminal record referred to OPD for investigation and determination.	Hearing Written appeal 8 NYCRR 28
3. Aircraft Operator	Federal Aviation Administration	Drug-related conviction renders one ineligible for license for 1 year and is grounds for suspension or revocation. Title 14 CFR 61.15	Become eligible for license one year after drug related offense. Title 14 CFR 61.15	Must have federal license GBL 241	N/A
4. Alcoholic Beverage Wholesaler/ Manufacturer/Retailer	State Liquor Authority	Mandatory bar for felonies and specific misdemeanors for licenses & employees. Applicant must disclose whether spouse has been convicted of crimes listed in §126. ABCL 110, 126, 3, 102	Bar for employees may be lifted by SLA permission, for employees & all others by pardon, C/GC, or C/R.	Fingerprinting Bonding Must disclose any pending criminal charges or convictions against applicant or applicant's spouse unless acquitted, dismissed, pardoned, C/GC, or C/R ABCL 110	Apply for hearing & review of denial of application by SLA to SLA. Subject to review by Supreme Ct. ABCL 121, 54
5. Ambulance Driver	SEE EMERGENCY MEDICAL TECHNICIAN				
6. Animal Health Permit	Dept of Agri & Mkts	Discretionary– application *may* be denied or revoked if convicted of a felony. A&M L 90-e		Good character and responsibility, ADBC A&M L 90-d	Notice and hearing A&M L 90-e

OCCUPATION	AGENCY	CRIMINAL RECORD RESTRICTIONS	REMOVAL OF CRIMINAL RECORD RESTRICTIONS	RELATED RESTRICTIONS	RIGHTS AND APPEAL PROCEDURES
7. Architect	State Ed Dept	None		Good moral character, ADBD Educ L §7304 *Any information about criminal record referred to OPD for investigation and determination.	Hearing Written appeal 8 NYCRR 28
8. Attorney	Committee on Character & Fitness of Applicants for Admission to the Bar	None		Good moral character CPLR §9404	N/A Must obtain permission from appellate division in which had filed in order to refile application. CPLR §9405
9. Baby Chick Seller	Dept of Agri & Mkts	None		None A&M L §175-n	N/A
10. Bail Bondsman (sic)	State Ins Dept	Mandatory– applicant *must* not have been convicted of any offense involving moral turpitude or of any crime. Ins L §6802(g)		Fingerprinting Good character & reputation Bonding Ins L §6802(g)	Art. 78 CPLR Ins L §2124
11. Barber	Dept of State	Discretionary– license *may* be suspended or revoked for one year if convicted of crime or offense involving moral turpitude or for habitual substance abuse. GBL §441	N/A	Good moral character GBL §434(B)	Revocation hearing
12. Barber Shop Owner	Dept of State	Discretionary– license *may* be suspended or revoked for one year if convicted of crime or offense involving moral turpitude or for habitual substance abuse. GBL §441		Good moral character GBL §438(3)	Revocation hearing

OCCUPATION	AGENCY	CRIMINAL RECORD RESTRICTIONS	REMOVAL OF CRIMINAL RECORD RESTRICTIONS	RELATED RESTRICTIONS	RIGHTS AND APPEAL PROCEDURES
13. Beer Brewer/ Wholesaler	SEE ALCOHOLIC BEVERAGE WHOLESALER				
14. Bingo Distributor/ Operator	State Racing & Wagering Bd NYC: Consumer Affairs	Bar for conviction of any crime. Exec L §435(2)(c)(1)	Bar may be lifted by pardon, C/GC, or C/R Exec L §435(2)(c)(1)	Good moral character No one who has been a professional gambler or gambling promoter Exec L §435(2)(c)(2)	Appeal to State Bingo Control Commission Exec L §435(1)(d)
15. Blasters (also: Lasers, Radiation & Crane Ops.)	Dept of Labor NYC: Fire Dept	None		May require: Bonding Fingerprinting GBL §483	N/A
16. Boxer/Wrestler	State Athletic Commission of Dept of State	Discretionary— may refuse to issue or revoke if convicted of a crime or if consorting with anyone convicted of a crime. Uncon L §8917		Fingerprinting Uncon L §8911 Character & fitness Uncon L §8912	N/A
17. Boxing/Wrestling: License to ALL Direct or Indirect Participants	SEE BOXER/ WRESTLER				
18. Bus Driver	Dept. of Motor Vehicles	Mandatory— felony bar for certain sex offenses and for certain vehicular offenses. V&T L §509-C	Bar may be waived if 5 years since release from sentence and (in case of felony) a C/R. V&T L §509-C	None	Art. 78 CPLR V&T L §263
19. Chauffeur	SEE TAXI DRIVER				

OCCUPATION	AGENCY	CRIMINAL RECORD RESTRICTIONS	REMOVAL OF CRIMINAL RECORD RESTRICTIONS	RELATED RESTRICTIONS	RIGHTS AND APPEAL PROCEDURES
20. Check Cashier	State Banking Dept	Discretionary— *may* be refused if convicted of a crime or if consorting with anyone who has been convicted of a crime. Mandatory— *must* not have been convicted of a felony. Banking L §369(6)	Both bars may be lifted by reversal of conviction, pardon or C/GC. Banking L §369(6)	Character & fitness Banking L §369(1)	N/A
21. Chiropractor	State Ed Dept	None		Good moral character, ADBD Educ L §6554(7) *Any information about criminal record referred to OPD for investigation and determination.	Hearing Written appeal 8 NYCRR 28
22. Civil Service Employee of NYC	NYC Dept of Citywide Admin Services	None		Satisfactory character and reputation NYC Civil Service Rules & Regulations §3.2.6	
23. Commercial Feed Mftr/ Distributor	Dept of Agri & Mkts	Discretionary— *may* be denied or revoked if convicted of felony, without subsequent pardon by the governor or other appropriate authority in the state or jurisdiction of the conduct or without a certificate of good conduct A&M L §129	Bar may be lifted by pardon or by C/GC. A&M L §129	Character & responsibility A&M L §129	Notice and hearing Art 78 CPLR A&M L §129-a
24. Controlled Substance Mftr/Dist.	Dept of Health	None	N/A	Must submit affidavit if ever convicted of drug offense. PHL §3312(2)(b) Good moral character PHL §3312(1)(a)	Within 30 days of denial of license may submit additional info or demand hearing PHL §3313(2)
25. Cosmetologist	SEE HAIRDRESSER				

OCCUPATION	AGENCY	CRIMINAL RECORD RESTRICTIONS	REMOVAL OF CRIMINAL RECORD RESTRICTIONS	RELATED RESTRICTIONS	RIGHTS AND APPEAL PROCEDURES
26. Dental Hygienist	State Ed Dept	None		Good moral character, ADBD Educ L §6609(7) *Any information about criminal record referred to OPD for investigation and determination.	Hearing Written appeal 8 NYCRR 28
27. Dentist	State Ed Dept	None		Good moral character, ADBD Educ L §6604(7) *Any information about criminal record referred to OPD for investigation and determination.	Hearing Written appeal 8 NYCRR 28
28. Deputy Sheriff	County Supervisor's Office	None		Fingerprinting County L §652(4)	N/A
29. Dietician	State Ed Dept	None Educ L §8004		None Educ L §8004	N/A
30. Disposal Plant or Transportation Service Operator	Dept of Agri & Mkts	Discretionary– *may* be barred, suspended or revoked if convicted of a felony. A&M L §96-z-3	Bar may be lifted by pardon or C/GC. A&M L §96-z-3	Character, ADBC A&M L §96-z-2	Notice and hearing Review if requested w/in 30 days of denial according to Art. 78 CPLR. A&M L §96-z-4
31. Dog Owner	Dept of Agri & Mkts	None		None A&M L §109	N/A
32. Dry Milk Importer	Dept of Agri & Mkts	None A&M L §258dd		Registration 1 NYCRR 13.2	N/A
33. Licensed Electrician	Dept of Buildings	Discretionary– *may* be suspended or revoked if convicted of a crime NYC Admin Code §27-3016(1)(vii)		Good moral character NYC Admin Code §27-3010	Notice & revocation hearing NYC Admin Code §27-3016(i)
34. Embalmer	SEE FUNERAL DIRECTOR				

OCCUPATION	AGENCY	CRIMINAL RECORD RESTRICTIONS	REMOVAL OF CRIMINAL RECORD RESTRICTIONS	RELATED RESTRICTIONS	RIGHTS AND APPEAL PROCEDURES
35. Emergency Medical Technician	State Emergency Medical Services Council	Mandatory bar for (i) certain felonies (e.g. murder, manslaughter, theft, drug offenses, robbery, fraud, assault, sexual abuse) and (ii) embezzlement. PHL §3005(8)	Bar waived if conviction does not demonstrate present danger. PHL §3005(8)	None PHL §3005(5)	N/A
36. Employment Agency Operator	Dept of Labor NYC: Consumer Affairs	None		Good moral character Fingerprinting GBL §173, 174	N/A
37. Engineer	State Ed Dept	None		Good moral character, ADBD Educ L §7206 *Any information about criminal record referred to OPD for investigation and determination.	Hearing Written appeal 8 NYCRR 28
38. Explosives Handler	Commissioner of Dept of Labor	Discretionary– *may* be denied or revoked if convicted of crime for which sentenced to serve one or more years in prison. Labor L §459(1)		Not confined as patient or inmate in institution for treatment of mental diseases Reliable Fingerprinting (may be waived if applicant has gun license) Labor L §458(4) &(7), §459(1)	Hearing Labor L §459.3
39. Farm Labor Contractor	Div of Labor Standards of Dept of Labor	Discretionary– *may* be denied or revoked if convicted of any crime or offense, except traffic violations. Labor L §212-a		Fingerprinting Labor L §212-a	Hearing Labor L §212-a
40. Farm Products Dealer	Dept of Agri & Mkts	None		Good character Bonding A&M L 248	Art 78 CPLR A&M L §250-h
41. Fertilizer Distributor	Dept of Agri & Mkts	None		None A&M L §146	N/A

OCCUPATION	AGENCY	CRIMINAL RECORD RESTRICTIONS	REMOVAL OF CRIMINAL RECORD RESTRICTIONS	RELATED RESTRICTIONS	RIGHTS AND APPEAL PROCEDURES
42. Firearms Carrier	Licensing Officer of City	Mandatory denial of applicant for felony and serious offenses. PL §400.00 Mandatory—automatic revocation if convicted of felony or serious offense while licensed. PL §400.00	N/A	Good moral character and never been confined to mental hospital or have history of mental illness. Fingerprinting PL §400.00	N/A
43. Firefighter	Fire Dept	Mandatory felony bar for applicants NYC Admin Code §15-103 Discretionary discipline or removal for conviction of any legal offense, conduct injurious to public peace or welfare, or immoral conduct, ADBC. NYC Admin Code §15-113	N/A	None	Right to public examination of charges for dismissal NYC Admin Code §15-113
44. Food Processing Plant Operator	Dept of Agri & Mkts	Discretionary— may be denied or revoked if convicted of a felony. A&M L §251-z-5(7)	N/A	Good character Bonding A&M L §251-z-3	Art 78 CPLR A&M L §251-z-6
45. Food Salvager	Dept of Agri & Mkts	Discretionary— may be denied, revoked or suspended if convicted of a crime. A&M L §220		Good character, ADBC A&M L §219	Art 78 CPLR A&M L §221
46. Frozen Dessert	Dept of Agri & Mkts	None		Character and experience A&M L §71-d	Art 78 CPLR A&M L §71-f
47. Funeral Director	Dept of Health	None for applicants Discretionary— may be revoked for conviction for crime. Automatically revoked for conviction of a felony. PHL §3450	License may be restored if granted a pardon or C/GC. PHL §3454	May be revoked for habitual drunkenness or addiction to narcotics. PHL §3450	Hearing PHL §3451 Art. 78 CPLR

OCCUPATION	AGENCY	CRIMINAL RECORD RESTRICTIONS	REMOVAL OF CRIMINAL RECORD RESTRICTIONS	RELATED RESTRICTIONS	RIGHTS AND APPEAL PROCEDURES
48. Furniture & Bedding Manufacturing	Dept of State	None		None GBL §388	N/A
49. Harbor Pilot	State Bd of Commissioners of Pilots	None		Good moral character & temperate habits Nav L §92	N/A
50. Hairdresser	Dept of State	None for applicants License *may* be revoked if convicted of any crime or offense involving moral turpitude or for habitual substance abuse. GBL §411		Freedom from infectious or communicable disease. Good moral character GBL §411	Revocation hearing & Denial hearing GBL §411
51. Hearing Aid Dealer	Dept of State	Revocation/suspension for conviction of any crime related to duties of the job.		Good character, reputation, & fitness GBL §790	May request hearing if denied. GBL §800
52. Horse Racing	State Racing & Wagering Bd	Discretionary— *may* be denied or revoked if convicted of a crime or for consorting with anyone convicted of a crime. RPMWBL §213(2)		Character and general fitness RPMWBL §213(2)	N/A
53. Insurance Securities Salesperson	State Ins Dept	None		Public interest Ins L §1204	Hearing Ins L §2103 Art 78 CPLR Ins L §2124
54. Insurance & Savings Bank Officers & Employees	State Ins Dept	None		Trustworthy and competent Ins L §2202(2)	Hearing Ins L §2103 Art 78 CPLR Ins L §2124

OCCUPATION	AGENCY	CRIMINAL RECORD RESTRICTIONS	REMOVAL OF CRIMINAL RECORD RESTRICTIONS	RELATED RESTRICTIONS	RIGHTS AND APPEAL PROCEDURES
55. Inspectors & Investigators for Dept of Agri	Dept of Agri & Mkts	None		Fingerprinting A&M L §11	N/A
56. Jockey	SEE HORSE RACING PERSONNEL				
57. Junk Dealer	Mayor's Office of City	Mandatory— applicant *must* not have been convicted of larceny or knowingly receiving stolen property. GBL §61	None	None	N/A
58. Land Surveyor	State Ed Dept	None		Good moral character, ADBD Educ L §7206-a(7) *Any information about criminal record referred to OPD for investigation and determination.	Hearing Written appeal 8 NYCRR 28
59. Liming Materials Seller	Dept of Agri & Mkts	None		None A&M L §142ee	Art 78 CPLR A&M L §142ee
60. Long-Shoreman (sic)	Waterfront Commission	Discretionary— registration *may* be denied or revoked if convicted of treason, murder, manslaughter, or of any felony or high misdemeanor. Uncon L §9829	Bar may be lifted by pardon. Uncon L §9829	None	Hearing Uncon L §9845
61. Masseur/Masseuse	State Ed Dept	None		Good moral character, ADBD Educ L §7804(6) *Any information about criminal record referred to OPD for investigation and determination.	Hearing Written appeal 8 NYCRR 28
62. Melloream Mftr	Dept of Agri & Mkts	None		None A&M L §50-g	N/A

OCCUPATION	AGENCY	CRIMINAL RECORD RESTRICTIONS	REMOVAL OF CRIMINAL RECORD RESTRICTIONS	RELATED RESTRICTIONS	RIGHTS AND APPEAL PROCEDURES
63. Midwife	State Ed Dept	None		Good moral character, ADBD Educ L §6955 *Any information about criminal record referred to OPD for investigation and determination.	Hearing Written appeal 8 NYCRR 28
64. Migrant Farm Worker	SEE FARM LABOR CONTRACTOR				
65. Milk Dealer	Dept of Agri & Mkts	Discretionary– *may* be denied, revoked or suspended if convicted of a felony. A&ML § 258-c(i)		Good character (No) acts injurious to public health Bonding A&ML §258-c	Notice and hearing A&ML §258-c Art 78 CPLR A&ML §258-d
66. Milk Tester/Weigher/ Grader	Dept of Agri & Mkts	None		Good moral character A&ML §57-a	N/A
67. Money Lender	State Banking Dept	None		Good character & general fitness Banking L §342	N/A
68. Money Transmitter	State Banking Dept	None		Good character & general fitness Banking L §642	Hearing Banking L §642
69. Notary Public	Dept of State	Mandatory– felony and specific misdemeanor (e.g. drug offenses) bars for applicants. Exec L §130		Good moral character Banking L §130 Exec L § 130	N/A
70. Nurse	State Ed Dept	None		Good moral character, ADBD -RN: Educ L §6905 -LPN: Educ L §6906 *Any information about criminal record referred to OPD for investigation and determination.	Hearing Written appeal 8 NYCRR 28

OCCUPATION	AGENCY	CRIMINAL RECORD RESTRICTIONS	REMOVAL OF CRIMINAL RECORD RESTRICTIONS	RELATED RESTRICTIONS	RIGHTS AND APPEAL PROCEDURES
71. Nursery (Trees) Stock Seller	Dept of Agri & Mkts	None		None A&M L §163-a	N/A
72. Nutritionist	SEE DIETICIAN				
73. Occupational Therapist	State Ed Dept	None		Good moral character, ADBD Educ L §7904 *Any information about criminal record referred to OPD for investigation and determination.	Hearing Written appeal 8 NYCRR 28
74. Opthalmic Dispenser	State Ed Dept	None		Good moral character, ADBD Educ L §7124 *Any information about criminal record referred to OPD for investigation and determination.	Hearing Written appeal 8 NYCRR 28
75. Optometrist	State Ed Dept	None		Good moral character, ADBD Educ L §7104 *Any information about criminal record referred to OPD for investigation and determination.	Hearing Written appeal 8 NYCRR 28
76. Pawn Broker	Mayor's Office or local licensing authority	None		Good character Bonding GBL §41	N/A
77. Pharmacist	State Ed Dept	None		Good moral character, ADBD Educ L §6805 *Any information about criminal record referred to OPD for investigation and determination.	Hearing Written appeal 8 NYCRR 28

OCCUPATION	AGENCY	CRIMINAL RECORD RESTRICTIONS	REMOVAL OF CRIMINAL RECORD RESTRICTIONS	RELATED RESTRICTIONS	RIGHTS AND APPEAL PROCEDURES
78. Physical Therapist	State Ed Dept	None		Good moral character, ADBD Educ L §6734 *Any information about criminal record referred to OPD for investigation and determination.	Hearing Written appeal 8 NYCRR 28
79. Physician	State Ed Dept	None		Good moral character, ADBD Educ L §6524 *Any information about criminal record referred to OPD for investigation and determination.	Hearing Written appeal 8 NYCRR 28
80. Physician's Assistant	State Ed Dept	None		Good moral character, ADBD Educ L §6541 *Any information about criminal record referred to OPD for investigation and determination.	Hearing Written appeal 8 NYCRR 28
81. Pier Superintendent/ Hiring Agent	Waterfront Commission	Mandatory— felony and specific misdemeanor (e.g. drug offenses) bar for applicants. Uncon L §9814 Discretionary—revocation for (i) conviction of felony or specific misdemeanor (e.g. drug offense) (ii) consorting with anyone convicted of such an offense or (iii) drug addiction or distribution. Uncon L §9818	Bar may be lifted if applicant has 5 years good conduct or by pardon. Uncon L §9814	Good character and integrity Uncon L §9814	Hearing Uncon L §9845
82. Plant/Soil Innoculant Seller	Dept of Agri & Mkts	None		None A&M L §147-b	Art 78 CPLR A&M L §147-g

OCCUPATION	AGENCY	CRIMINAL RECORD RESTRICTIONS	REMOVAL OF CRIMINAL RECORD RESTRICTIONS	RELATED RESTRICTIONS	RIGHTS AND APPEAL PROCEDURES
83. Licensed Plumber	Dept of Buildings	None		Good moral character NYC Admin Code §26-133 Revocation for poor moral character that adversely reflects on fitness to conduct plumbing business NYC Admin Code §26-151	Revocation hearing NYC Admin Code §26-151
84. Podiatrist	State Ed Dept	None		Good moral character, ADBD Educ L §7004 *Any information about criminal record referred to OPD for investigation and determination.	Hearing Written appeal 8 NYCRR 28
85. Police Officer	Police Dept	Mandatory— permanent felony bar NYC Admin Code §14-109		None	N/A
86. Private Investigator (and employees)	Dept of State	Mandatory— felony and specific misdemeanor bar (e.g. drug offenses, buying/receiving/possessing stolen property, unlawful entry) for applicants. GBL §74 License suspended if convicted of crime. GBL §74	Bar may be lifted by pardon or C/GC. GBL §74	Bonding Fingerprinting Good character, competency, honesty and integrity Criminal history investigated GBL §§72, 81, 74	Hearing GBL §79
87. Psychologist	Dept of State	None		Good moral character, ADBD Educ L §7603 *Any information about criminal record referred to OPD for investigation and determination.	Hearing Written appeal 8 NYCRR 28
88. Public Adjuster	State Ins Dept	Mandatory— felony and specific misdemeanor bar for convictions involving fraudulent or dishonest practices. Ins L §2108(d)(3)&(4)	Bar may be lifted by pardon or C/GC. Ins L §2108(d)(3)&(4)	Trustworthy and competent Fingerprinting Ins L §2107, 2108(d)(2)&(5)	Hearing Ins L §2108 Art 78 CPLR Ins L §2124

OCCUPATION	AGENCY	CRIMINAL RECORD RESTRICTIONS	REMOVAL OF CRIMINAL RECORD RESTRICTIONS	RELATED RESTRICTIONS	RIGHTS AND APPEAL PROCEDURES
89. Race Track Worker	SEE HORSE RACING PERSONNEL				
90. Radiologist	Bureau of Environmental Radiation Protection	Suspension/revocation if guilty of crime involving moral turpitude Forfeiture of license if convicted of any crime considered a felony in New York PHL § 3510	Forfeiture may be lifted by pardon or C/GC PHL § 3510	Good moral character PHL §3505	Hearing PHL § 3511 Art 78 CPLR
91. Real Estate Broker/ Salesperson	Secretary of State	Mandatory— *must* not have been convicted of a felony. Real Prop L §440-a	Bar may be lifted by pardon or C/GC. Real Prop L §440-a	Trustworthiness Real Prop L §441	Hearing Real Prop L §441-e Art 78 CPLR Real Prop L §441-f
92. Refrigerator Warehouse and/or Locker Plant Operator	Dept of Agri & Mkts	None		Good character, fiscal responsibility & competency ADBC A&M L §231	Art 78 CPLR A&M L §232
93. Sanitation Worker	Sanitation Dept	Discretionary— *may* be punished or dismissed for conviction of any legal offense, conduct injurious to public peace or welfare, or immoral conduct, ADBC NYC Admin Code § 16-106		None	Opportunity to give explanation before punishment meted out. NYC Admin Code § 16-106
94. Scrap Processor	Mayor's Office	None		None GBL §69-f	N/A
95. Securities Broker Dealer Salesperson	Dept of Law	None		Must disclose criminal record. GBL §359-e(3)(a)(b) Fingerprinting GBL §359-e(12)	N/A

OCCUPATION	AGENCY	CRIMINAL RECORD RESTRICTIONS	REMOVAL OF CRIMINAL RECORD RESTRICTIONS	RELATED RESTRICTIONS	RIGHTS AND APPEAL PROCEDURES
96. Security Guard	Dept of State	Mandatory— felony and certain misdemeanors if related to functions of job. GBL §89 Registration suspended if convicted of enumerated crimes. GBL §89	Bar may be lifted by pardon or C/Relief from Disabilities. GBL §89	Fingerprinting Good character and fitness Criminal history investigated GBL §§89	Hearing GBL §89
97. Shorthand Reporter (Certified)	State Ed Dept	None		Good moral character, ADBD Educ L §7504(7) *Any information about criminal record referred to OPD for investigation and determination.	Hearing Written appeal 8 NYCRR 28
98. Social Worker (Certified)	State Ed Dept	None		Good moral character, ADBD Educ L §7704(7) *Any information about criminal record referred to OPD for investigation and determination.	Hearing Written appeal 8 NYCRR 28
99. Speech Pathologist	State Ed Dept	None		Good moral character, ADBD Educ L 8206 *Any information about criminal record referred to OPD for investigation and determination.	Hearing Written appeal 8 NYCRR 28
100. Stevedore	Waterfront Commission	SAME AS PIER SUPERINTENDENT. Uncon L §9821		Good character & integrity Uncon L §9821	Hearing Uncon L §9845

OCCUPATION	AGENCY	CRIMINAL RECORD RESTRICTIONS	REMOVAL OF CRIMINAL RECORD RESTRICTIONS	RELATED RESTRICTIONS	RIGHTS AND APPEAL PROCEDURES
101. Taxi Driver	Dept of Motor Vehicles	Same as for drivers licenses generally. Mandatory revocation for convictions for certain vehicular offenses. Mandatory suspension for convictions for certain drug-related felonies and misdemeanors and for assault against traffic enforcement agent. Permissive suspension and revocation for any felony conviction. V&T L §510		Permissive suspensions for intoxication or use of drugs and for commitment to institution under jurisdiction of Dept of Mental Hygiene V&T L 510 Good moral character Fingerprinting No drug or alcohol addiction NYC Admin Code §19-505	Art 78 CPLR V&T L §263 Revocation hearing for city license NYC Admin Code §19-505(L)
102. Teacher	State Dept of Ed	None		Good moral character, ADBD Fingerprinting Educ L §§ 3012, 3020, 2590-h(20).	Hearing Educ L §2590-g
103. Theatre Ticket Reseller	City or County Licensing Commission	None		Good moral character ACA L §25.03 Bonding ACA L §25.07	N/A
104. Truck Driver	Dept of Motor Vehicles	Must report once per year all convictions for violations of vehicle laws & ordinances other than those involving parking. V&T L §509-t		None	Art. 78 CPLR V&T L §263
105. Undertaker	SEE FUNERAL DIRECTOR				
106. Veterinarian	State Ed Dept	None		Good moral character, ADBD Educ L §6704 *Any information about criminal record referred to OPD for investigation and determination.	Hearing Written appeal 8 NYCRR 28
107. Weighmaster	Dept of Agri & Mkts	None		Good character A&M L §195	Hearing A&M L §195

OCCUPATION	AGENCY	CRIMINAL RECORD RESTRICTIONS	REMOVAL OF CRIMINAL RECORD RESTRICTIONS	RELATED RESTRICTIONS	RIGHTS AND APPEAL PROCEDURES
108. X-Ray Technician and X-Ray Therapy Technician	SEE RADIOLOGIST				

APPENDIX A - <u>ABBREVIATIONS</u>

ABCL	Alcoholic Beverage Control Law
ACA L	Arts and Cultural Affairs Law
ADBC	As Determined by Commissioner
ADBD	As Determined by Department
A&M L	Agriculture and Markets Law
CFR	Code of Federal Regulations
C/GC	Certificate of Good Conduct
Cor L	Correction Law
CPA	Certified Public Accounting
CPLR	Civil Practice Law and Rules
C/R	Certificate of Relief from Disabilities
Educ L	Education Law
Exec L	Executive Law
GBL	General Business Law
Ins L	Insurance Law
LPN	Licensed Practical Nurse
N/A	No Applicable Statute
NYCRR	New York Code of Rules and Regulations
OPD	Office of Professional Discipline
PHL	Public Health Law
PL	Penal Law
RN	Registered Nurse
RPMWBL	Racing, Pari-Mutual Wagering, and Breeding Law
Uncon L	Unconsolidated Laws
V&T L	Vehicle and Traffic Law

Appendix E

IRS Publications and Forms

U.S. Department of the Treasury
Internal Revenue Service
Eastern Area Distribution Center
P.O. Box 85074
Richmond, VA 23261-5074

PUBLICATIONS:

1635	Understanding Your EIN (Employer's Identification Number)
538	Accounting Periods and Methods
505	Tax Withholding and Estimated Tax
542	Depositing Taxes
533	Self-Employment Tax
527	Real Estate Investor
946	How to Depreciate Property
587	Business Use of Your Home
463	Travel, Entertainment, Gift and Car Expenses
535	Business Expenses
557	Tax-Exempt Status for Your Organization
334	Tax Guide for Small Business (Sole Proprietorship)
541	Partnerships
542	Corporations
560	Retirement Plans for Small Business
15	Circular E, Employer's Tax Guide

15A   Employer's Supplement Tax Guide

FORMS:

1040   U.S. Individual Tax Return
1065   U.S. Return of Partnership Income
2253   Election By a Small Business Corporation (S
                   Corporation)
1120   U.S. Corporation Income Tax Return
1120S   U.S. Income Tax Return for an S Corporation
8829   Expenses for Business Use of Your Home
8109   Federal Tax Deposit Coupon
8881   Credit for Small Employer Pension Plan Start-Up
                   Costs
941   Employer's Quarterly Federal Tax Return
1023   Application for Recognition of Exemption Under
                   501 (c)(3) of the IRC
8178   User Fee for Exempt Organization Determination
                   Letter Request
990   Return of Organization Exempt from Income Tax
SS-4   Application for Employer Identification Number

Schedule C   Business Profit or Loss
Schedule SE   Self-Employment Tax
Schedule K-1   Partner's Share of Income, Credits, Deductions

Business Tax Deductions

A

Abandonment of property used for business purposes

Accounting and auditing expenses, such as:

    Auditing of your books and accounts

    Costs of bookkeeping

    Costs of tax strategy preparation

    Costs of preparing and filing any tax returns

    Costs of investigation of any tax returns

    Costs of defense against any IRS or state agency audits or challenges

Accounts receivable, worthless

Achievement awards—requires plan

    Longevity award

    Safety award

    Sales award

Advances made to employees or salespeople where repayment is not expected

Advances to employees canceled as bonus

Advertising expenses, such as:

    Premiums given away

    Advertising in:

        Newspaper

        Magazine

        Radio

Other media

Prizes and other expenses in holding contests or exhibitions

Contributions to various organizations for advertising purposes

Cost of displays, posters, etc. to attract customers

Publicity—generally speaking, all costs including entertainment, music, etc.

Christmas present to customers or prospects—de minimis rule

Alterations to business property, if minor

Amortization

Attorney's fees and other legal expenses involving:

Tax strategy

Drafting of agreements, resolutions, minutes, etc.

Defense of claims against you

Collection actions taken against others

Any other business-related legal activity

Auto expenses for business purposes, such as:

Damage to auto not covered by insurance

Gasoline

Oil

Repairs and maintenance

Washing and waxing

Garage rent

Interest portion of payments

Insurance premiums such as fire, theft, collision, liability, etc.

Lease payment

License plate

Driver's license fee

Depreciation

Wages of chauffeur

Section 179 deduction, for qualified vehicle

B

Bad debts—if previously taken into income

Baseball/softball/soccer team equipment for business publicity

Board and room to employee:
   All meals and lodging if for employer's benefit
   Temporary housing assignment
Board meetings
Bonuses as additional compensation to employees
Bookkeeping services
Building expenses, used for business, such as:
   Repairs to building
   Janitorial service
   Painting
   Interest on mortgage
   Taxes on property
   Water
   Rubbish removal
   Depreciation of building
   Heating
   Lighting
   Landscaping
Burglary losses not covered by insurance
Business, cost of operating office
Business taxes—except federal income taxes

C
Cafeteria plan—requires written plan
Capital asset sale—losses
Car and taxi fares
Casualty damages, such as:
   Bombardment
   Fire
   Storm
   Hurricane
   Drought
   Forest fire
   Freezing of property
   Impairment or collapse of property

Ice
Heat
Wind
Rain
Charitable contributions
Checking account bank charges
Child care—requires written plan
Children's salaries
Christmas presents to employees, customers and prospects for
    advertising or publicity purposes, or goodwill, or if customary
    in the trade
Collection expenses including attorney's charges
Commissions on sales of securities by dealers in securities
Commissions paid to agents
Commissions paid to employees for business purposes
Commissions paid to salesmen
Condemnation expenses
Contributions (deductible if made to organization founded for the
    following purposes, subject to some limitations):
    Religious
    Charitable
    Scientific
    Literary
    Educational
    Prevention of cruelty to children and animals
Convention expenses, cost of attending conventions
Cost of goods
Credit report costs

D

Daycare facility
Depletion
Depreciation
Discounts allowed to customers
Dues paid to:
    Better Business Bureau
    Chamber of commerce
    Trade associations
    Professional societies
    Technical societies
    Protective services association

E

Education assistance—requires written plan
Embezzlement loss not covered by insurance
Employee welfare expenses, such as:
    Dances
    Entertainment
    Outings
    Christmas parties
    Shows or plays
Endorser's loss
Entertainment expenses
Equipment, minor replacements
Equipment purchases—may require capitalization and
    depreciation
Equipment repairs
Exhibits and displays, to publicize your products
Expenses of any kind directly chargeable to business income,
    such as:
    Renting of storage space
    Safe deposit boxes
    Upkeep of property
    Books to record income and expenses or investment income

Experimental and research expenses

F
Factoring
Fan mail expenses
Fees for passports necessary while traveling on business
Fees to accountants
Fees to agents
Fees to brokers
Fees to investment counsel
Fees to professionals for services rendered
Fees to technicians
Fire loss
Forfeited stock
Freight charges

G
Gifts to customers—limit $75
Gifts to organized institutions, such as:
    Charitable
    Literary
    Educational
    Religious
    Scientific
Group term insurance on employees' lives
Guarantor's loss

H
Health insurance
Heating expense
Hospitals, contributions to

I
Improvements, provided they are minor
Insurance premiums paid

Interest on loans of all kinds for business purposes, such as:
    On loans
    On notes
    On mortgages
    On bonds
    On tax deficiencies
    On installment payments of auto, furniture, etc.
    On margin account with brokers
    Bank discount on note is deductible as interest
Inventory loss due to damages
Investment counsel fees

L
Lawsuit expenses
Legal costs
    In defense of your business
    In settlement of cases
    Payment of damages
License fees
Lighting
Living quarter furnished employees for business's benefit
Lobbying costs
Losses, deductible if connected with your business or profession,
    such as:
    Abandoned property
    Accounts receivable
    Auto damage caused by fire, theft, heat, storm, etc.
    Bad debts
    Bank closed
    Bonds
    Buildings—damaged
    Burglary
    Business ventures
    Capital assets
    Casualties: fire, theft, heat, storm, etc.

Damages to property or assets
Deposit forfeiture, on purchase of property
Drought
Embezzlements
Equipment abandoned
Forced sale or exchange
Foreclosures
Forfeitures
Freezing
Goodwill
Loans not collectible
Theft
Transactions entered into for profits

M

Maintenance of business property
Maintenance of office, store, warehouse, showroom, etc.
Maintenance of rented premises
Management costs
Materials
Meals, subject to limitation
Membership dues
Merchandise
Messenger service
Moving cost
Musician expenses

N

Net operating loss—may be carried back to previous years' income
    for refund and/or forward against future years' income
Newspapers

O
Office expenses, including:
    Wages
    Supplies
    Towel service
    Heating and lighting
    Telephone and telegraph
    Repairs
    Refurnishing, minor items
    Decorating
    Painting
Office rent
Office rent—portion of home used for business
Office stationery and supplies

P
Passport fees
Pension plans—must be properly drawn
Periodicals
Physical fitness center
Plotting of land for sale
Postage
Professional society dues
Property depreciation
Property maintenance
Property repairs
Publicity expenses

R
Real estate expenses of rental or investment property, including:
    Taxes of property
    Insurance
    Janitorial services
    Repairing
    Redecorating

    Painting
    Depreciation
    Supplies
    Tools
    Legal expenses involving leases, tenants or property
    Bookkeeping
    Property management
    Utilities
    Commissions to secure tenants
    Maintenance—heating, lighting, etc.
    Advertising for tenants
    Cost of manager's unit, if on site and at employer's
    convenience
Rebates on sales
Refunds on sales
Rent settlement—cancel lease
Rental property expense, such as:
    Advertising of vacant premises
    Commissions to secure tenant
    Billboards and signs
Rent collection expense
Rents paid, such as:
    Business property
    Parking facilities
    Safe deposit boxes
    Taxes paid by tenant for landlord
    Warehouse and storage charges
Repairing of business property, such as:
    Alterations, provided they are not capital additions
    Casualty damages, replaced, provided they are not capital
    additions
    Cleaning
    Minor improvements
    Painting
    Redecorating

Repairing of furniture, fixtures, equipment, machinery, and
buildings
Roof repairs
Royalties

S
Safe deposit box rental
Safe or storage rental
Salaries (including bonuses, commissions, pensions, management
fees)
Sample room
Selling expenses, such as:
Commissions and bonuses as prizes
Discounts
Entertainment
Prizes offered in contests
Publicity and promotion costs
Rebates
Services, professional or other necessary for conduct of business
Social Security taxes paid by employers
Stationery and all other office supplies used
Subscriptions to all trade, business or professional periodicals
Supplies, office or laboratory

T
Taxes, all taxes paid except federal income taxes, such as:
City gross receipts tax
City sales tax
State gross receipts tax
State sales tax
State unemployment insurance tax
Federal Social Security tax
State income tax
State unincorporated business tax
Real estate tax

Tangible property tax
Intangible property tax
Custom, import or tariff tax
License tax
Stamp taxes
Any business tax, as a rule
Auto registration tax
Safe deposit tax
Membership dues tax
Gasoline tax
Admission tax
Telephone and telegraphs
Traveling expenses (includes: meals, taxi fare, rail fare, airfare, tips, telephone, telegrams, laundry and cleaning, entertainment for business purposes)

U
Unemployment compensation taxes paid by employer
Uniforms furnished to employees

W
Wages
Workmen's compensation fund contributions

INDEX

A. C. T., 83-84

Accion International, 203

Accounting, 37, 160-161, 163, 211, 255, 257

Accounting Periods, 255

Accounts, 59, 62, 64, 66-68, 137, 139-142, 145, 150, 161-163, 257, 263

Accrual System, 160-161

Advertising, 131-132, 257-258, 260, 266

Advisors, 28, 105, 123, 125, 143, 211

American Association of Individual Investors (AAII), 73

Amortization, 141, 258

APR (Annual Percentage Rate), 149

Arbitration, 100, 188

Articles of Incorporation, 123

Articles of Organization, 117

Ashe, Arthur, 40

Ashoka, 120

Asset, 25, 81-82, 140, 143, 259

Asset Mapping, 81-82

Auditing, 257

Baisden, Michael, 31

Bankrate.com, 67

Banks, 50, 66, 71, 138-140, 145-146, 148, 169

Bauer Financial, 67

Berkowitz, David, 95

Better Business Bureau, 261

Bonds, 15, 49, 51, 62, 68-72, 115, 138, 141, 263

Bookkeeping, 159-160, 165, 257, 259, 266

Breach of Contract, 182, 188

Broker, 72-73, 90

Business Expenses, 122, 167, 173-174, 255-256, 258-259

Business Financing, 104, 137, 211

Business Infrastructure Checklist, 78

Business Plan Components, 104

Business Structures, 107-109, 111, 115, 170

Business Tax Deductions, 15, 174, 256-257

Bylaws, 123

C-Corporations, 110-111, 171

Cash Ledger, 164-165

CDs, 66-68

Certificate of Good Conduct, 93-94

Certificate of Incorporation, 117-118

Certificate of Limited Partnership, 116

Certificate of Relief, 93-94

Certified Public Accountant (CPA), 168

Change, 7, 21-25, 27-32, 34-35, 43, 52, 54, 75, 77, 93, 120, 131, 176, 197

Characteristics Of A Successful Entrepreneur, 34-35

Charities, 120, 122

Checking Account, 260

Civil Disabilities, 93

Collateral, 49, 139-141, 148-149

Commissions, 73, 168, 260, 266-267

Common Stock, 69

Compound Interest, 59-61

Contract Basics, 181

Contracts, 122, 179, 181-183

Copyrights, 190, 193

Corporations, 68, 70, 107, 109-111, 114, 120-121, 124, 148, 171-172, 216, 223, 255

Court of Claims, 188

CPA, 168, 171

Credit, 50, 53, 65, 68, 137, 139-140,
    142, 145, 147-151, 155-157,
    160-161, 163-164, 256, 260
Credit Cards, 53, 137, 147-150, 161
Credit Report, 147, 150-151, 156, 260
Crime Victims Board, 95
Cultural Equation, 30

Debit, 163-164
Deductions, 15, 167, 173-174, 256-257
Department of Taxation, 117-118
Depositing Taxes, 169, 255
Depreciation, 258-259, 261, 265-266
Direct Marketing Association, 204
Direct Selling Association, 204
Direct Stock Purchase Plans, 73
Directory of DRIPs, 73
Discretionary Legal Bars, 90
Discretionary Relief From Forfeitures, 93
Dividend Reinvestment Programs, 73
Doing Business As (DBA), 116
Donations, 115, 122
Dow Jones Industrial Average, 71
Drayton, Bill, 120
DRIPs, 73
DSPs, 73

EIN, 124, 255
Enron, 37
Equifax, 151, 156
Estimated Tax, 169-171, 255
Executive Summary, 104, 141
Expand Your Context, 28-29
Expenses, 56, 71, 121-122, 159, 161,
    167, 173-174, 177, 255-268
Experian, 151, 156

Factoring, 140, 262
Failure As Teacher, 99
Fair Credit Billing Act, 157
FICO Score, 155
Filing Taxes, 167-174
Firstrade Securities, 72

Folsom, Jan, 11, 52
Folsom, Mark, 11, 52

G. E. D., 83, 119
Gangsta, 29
General Ledger, 164
General Partnership, 109-110, 112, 116
Getting Started, 72
Goldman Sachs, 86, 269
Guerrilla Marketing, 210

Hilliard, Landon, 85
Hiring, 101, 125, 168
Home-Based Business, 89, 176, 211

Identifying Your Niche, 127
Income Tax, 94, 106, 111-112, 114,
    167-172, 256, 267
Income Tax Withholding, 169
Increase Your Content, 28
Independent Sector, 120
Initial Public Offering, 110
Inmates Teaching Entrepreneurship &
    Mentoring (I.T.E.M.), 85
Intellectual Property, 189-190
Interest, 56, 58-61, 65-68, 70, 77, 80,
    93-94, 105, 112-113, 121-122,
    138-140, 145-149, 156-157, 180,
    258-259, 263
Internet, 70, 106, 128, 132-133
Inventory, 42, 47, 81, 139, 142, 263
Investing, 14, 16-17, 42-44, 50, 57-58,
    62-64, 68-69, 71-72, 196
IOUs, 70
IPO, 110

Journals, 161-162

Kauffman Foundation, 203
King, Don, 25
Kiyosaki, Robert T., 28, 207

La Cloche, Marc, 91
Ledgers, 161-163
Legal Forms, 183
Lenders, 104-105, 111, 143, 147, 150-151, 155
Leverage Your Vision, 17, 75
Liability, 25, 108, 110-111, 113-114, 117, 133, 167, 170, 176-177, 258
Library of Congress, 194
Licenses, 90, 92-93, 168
Licensing, 90-94, 190, 218, 231
Life Insurance, 137, 176-177
Limited Liability Company (LLC), 108, 110, 113, 170
Limited Partnership (LP), 110, 112
Loans, 53, 56, 68, 96, 138-141, 143, 145-147, 155, 203, 263-264
Lobbying, 122, 205, 263
Long-Term Goals, 54, 56, 108

Malcolm X, 26
Management, 34, 42-43, 71, 104-105, 108-109, 111-114, 125-126, 141-142, 159, 209, 264, 266-267
Mancuso, Joseph, 34, 212
Market, 34, 46-47, 50, 63, 67-68, 71-72, 83, 101, 106, 119, 122, 127-129, 131-133, 141-142, 145-146, 189-190
Market Research, 106, 128-129
Marketing, 41, 85, 100, 104, 106, 122, 127, 130-132, 134, 159, 193, 204, 210
Mariotti, Steve, 9, 11, 83-84, 86, 97, 128, 207, 209, 269
Medicare Taxes, 168-169
Mendez, Dr. Garry A., 11, 30
Mentoring, 76, 83, 85-86, 97, 120, 269
Micro Steps, 79-80
Micro-credit, 143
Money Market Accounts (MMA), 68
Mutual Funds, 15, 62, 71-72, 141

National Association of Investors Corporation (NAIC), 73
National Business Incubation Association (NBIA), 205
National Federation of Independent Business (NFIB), 206
National Foundation for Teaching Entrepreneurship (NFTE), 8, 83, 85, 269
National Trust for the Development of African-American Men (TNT), 30
New York State Occupational Licensing Survey, 231
NGOs, 120
No-Load Stocks, 73
Nonprofit Corporation, 111, 115, 118, 121

Partnership Agreement, 109
Partnerships, 108, 110, 146, 167, 255
Patent and Trademark Office (PTO), 190, 192
Patents, 190-193
Posting, 163-164
Preferred Stock, 69
Premiums, 147, 175, 257-258, 262
Principal, 59-60, 138-140, 147
Prison Entrepreneurship Program (PEP), 96
Product, 27, 69, 101-102, 127-128, 130-131, 133, 177, 193
Profits, 109, 111, 113, 121, 139, 168, 264
Promotions, 131-133
Property, 51, 91, 93, 95, 110, 141, 168, 177, 189-190, 255, 257-259, 261, 263-266, 268
Provisional Patent, 191
Publicity, 258, 260, 265, 267

Receipts, 54-55, 160, 267
Registering Your Business, 115, 193
Regular C-Corporation, 110, 114, 117
Repairing Credit Errors, 156
Retire Young, Retire Rich, 28, 207

Retirement Plans, 105, 255
Return on Investment (ROI), 146
Rich Dad, Poor Dad, 26, 28, 207
Rohr, Catherine, 96
Royalties, 190, 267
Rule, Sheila Rosita, 11

S-Corporation, 111, 114-115, 117, 170
Savings Account, 54, 58, 64-67, 150
Schedule C, 169, 256
Schedule E, 170
Schedule K-1, 256
Schedule SE, 169-170, 256
Scott, Laurie, 84
Securities, 37, 68, 71-73, 110, 146, 260
Securities and Exchange Commission
    (SEC), 110
Self-Employment Tax, 168-170, 255-256
Service Corps of Retired Executives
    (SCORE), 126, 174
Shareholders, 69, 110-111, 114, 121, 176
Shares, 69, 72-73, 110, 114-115
Simple Interest, 59-60
Small Business Administration (SBA),
    126
Small Claims Court, 188
SMART, 45-46, 50, 177
Social Entrepreneurship, 119-120
Social Security, 16, 150, 156, 168-169,
    267
Sole Proprietorship, 109, 111, 116, 169,
    177, 255
Son of Sam Law, 95-96

SS-4 Application, 256
Stocks, 15, 49, 51, 62, 68-73, 115, 141

Taking Baby Steps, 78
Tax Credits, 167, 171, 173
Tax Deductions, 15, 167, 173-174,
    256-257
Tax Withholding, 169, 255
Tax-Exempt Status, 115, 118, 122-124,
    255
Taxable Income, 172-174
Taxes, 94, 120-121, 167-171, 173-175,
    211, 255, 259, 265-268
TD Ameritrade, 72
The Ten Things Every Student Should
    Know, 85
Time Management, 42-43
Trademark Office, 190, 192-193
Trademarks, 190, 192-193
Transactions, 64, 161-163, 264
Transitional Services Program, 197
Travolta, John, 24

Unique Selling Proposition (USP), 129
Utility Patents, 190-192

Values, 29-30, 42-43, 53-54
Veribank, 145

Web Sites, 57, 77, 131-132, 212
Whitehead, John C., 84, 85
Whoodini, 31

ABOUT THE AUTHOR

JOE ROBINSON HAS BEEN teaching personal finance and entrepreneurship to incarcerated men since 1995. He is a certified instructor of Inmates Teaching Entrepreneurship & Mentoring (ITEM), a program he founded with Steve Mariotti, president and founder of the National Foundation for Teaching Entrepreneurship (NFTE). ITEM trains prison inmates to teach their children and fellow incarcerated men the basics of business ownership.

Joe tapped into the power of his own entrepreneurial gifts after he was incarcerated in 1992 for a crime that had its roots in the illegal drug business he operated. His appetite for legitimate business was whet as he read the business pages of newspapers that other prisoners discarded. He built his own business library by trading cigarettes for books, and he eventually became so knowledgeable that he grew to be the go-to person for fellow incarcerated men seeking information and guidance about entrepreneurship. His work has been recognized and supported by several current and former Wall Street executives—including Mr. Mariotti and John Whitehead, a former head of Goldman Sachs—who, at Joe's urging, have gone into prison to teach entrepreneurship to incarcerated men.

Joe and his wife, Sheila Rule, have two wonderful sons, Sean Rule and Joseph Brown.